Before The
"I Do's"
Seven Essential Conversations.

Lee A. Bowers, Ph.D

ISBN 978-0-9960536-0-0

Table of Contents

In Appreciation

To Amy, Caryn, Paul, and Beth - for your great input, ideas, insightfulness, and overall support for this project. Thanks so very much.

"Marriage is the alliance between two people;
one of whom never remembers birthdays,
and the other, who never forgets..."

Ogden Nash

Dedication

This book is dedicated to the many people who have passed through the doors of my office in my 30 plus years of practice as a psychotherapist and psychologist. It is dedicated to friends, family, and yes, even "exes." For the glimpses you've shared with me into your most intimate relationships, I feel privileged and honored. Much of what is condensed into this book, I learned from you. Thank you – and may you all continue to grow in the most happy and loving relationships.

The couples you will read about in this book and the issues they have struggled with are, for the most part, composites. The stories are compiled to best illustrate a typical issue or common problem. Occasionally an actual situation is used, but always with identifying information changed to protect the privacy of the people involved.

One final note about use of the word "marriage." I use this word as a term of convenience, rather than a legal definition. The reference applies to any long-term committed relationship between two consenting adults; whether or not it has been blessed by religious and/or state authorities.

Lee A. Bowers, Ph.D.
Villanova, PA   2014

Introduction

I f there is magic in our relationships, it is in our ability to love. Love is indeed a mystery, one that inspires respect and gratitude; but love is not only about this mystery, and love is not necessarily out of our control.

To be sure, in the beginning of any love relationship, there is an overwhelming sense of well-being and giddiness. As the relationship deepens, the initial stage of love is replaced with deeper bonds of commitment to honoring each other and the love you share, along with the everyday work of building a life together. This enduring, more practical love is a conscious choice.

Inevitably, the greatest drawback to healthy communication is not lack of honesty, but the unexamined, preconceived notions that many people bring into marriage. Such notions can be derived from the media, from varied experiences of early family life, and from all the hopes and expectations that surround what it means to love and be loved.

This book is intended to help lovers of all ages, from all walks of life, to not only select the best possible partner, but also to explore the healthiest possible relationship path with that partner. Through brief summaries of real stories from actual clients

I've worked with over the last 30 years, this book will share with you some very clear and simple steps that will change the way people approach partner selection and committed love.

Terri's Story

It's been about three decades since I did an internship in marriage and family therapy at a community mental health agency in Houston, Texas. But after all that time, I still remember Terri. I was struck by her circumstances and her story. Terri has been forever burned in my memory.

Probably most disturbing is that, although her situation was extreme, in some ways Terri's story demonstrates the norm more than the exception. Her story illustrates how little thought goes into relationships that are most essential to our well-being, bonds that are meant to be supportive and loving.

Terri was an abused wife. She married her high school boyfriend while still in her teens. Some five years later, she had seen more emergency rooms than most people experience in a lifetime; suffering broken bones, disfigurement, and numerous verbal threats to her life. Terri had been beaten unconscious on more than one occasion.

As I was gathering historical information in our first session, the thing that amazed me most was that Terri knew long before she married Tom that he was prone to violent outbursts. In fact, she'd already accumulated many bruises before their wedding.

Introduction

"Why?" I asked. "Why would you marry someone who would do such things to you?" From the outside looking in, the question is certainly perplexing, yet many people choose to stay with mates who do not nurture or support them in a loving manner. While there may not always be physical abuse as in Terri's case, millions of couples settle for an unhappy union that deprives one or the other of the support, communication, and nurturing they crave.

People sometimes cling to these relationships like life's breath itself. Some couples will constantly argue and bicker, while others resign themselves to a life of stony silence. Why do these people stay? More importantly, why do they marry people in the first place who (apparently) don't share their same basic values and approach to life? Such fundamental red flags should be obvious, but Terri's response was one that I would hear countless times over the years... "I love him," was her only reply.

Over and over, I heard about "how wonderful he is when he isn't being violent." Over and over, Terri professed her deep love for a man who ultimately took her to the brink of death.

The field of psychology has numerous explanations for why people stay in abusive relationships. This usually applies to women, but not always. Many come from abusive families and see violent behavior as the norm. Others have severely low self-esteem and believe what they've been told – that they deserve the abuse. Drugs and/or alcohol are often involved. Strong religious beliefs can stand in the way; especially those that discourage divorce, or view the husband as final arbiter in any disagreement. Another factor is not wanting children subjected to the difficulties of divorce. Finally, especially during difficult financial times, not having the monetary means to leave is often an issue.

While any or all of these sociological explanations can make sense, they did not fit for Terri's situation. None of them explained the fact that her only explanation was her repeated response of "I love him." What is it about love that blinds us and can turn even the most intelligent, well rounded and successful people into obsessive and miserable human beings? Why are otherwise healthy individuals reluctant to leave a toxic relationship and search for a better life?

In a word, the answer is - hormones. Hormones are the "crack" of love. OK, it doesn't all come down to hormones, because the real workhorse in any relationship is love; but it's hormones that give us that giddy, sick in the stomach, obsessive feeling, and it's hormones that make it so hard to leave, even when we know we should.

There is no doubt that falling in love feels fabulous. New love creates a biochemical high that lasts (on average) about 18 months. During that sweet spot of time, sounds are clearer and colors are richer. No matter what problems a job, family or money may present, all seems and *feels* right in the world. New love feels so good that we want to focus all our energy on staying in that amazingly wonderful state of being. We may think what we are feeling at the time is chemistry, and there is some scientific evidence that when falling in love, we are in fact victims of a biochemical reaction.

Introduction

As predictable, clinical and unromantic as a biochemical reaction may sound, it is worth bringing to light in order to gain understanding. When you step back from a relationship for just a second and allow the left-brain to take over, you may unveil some things about yourself and your partner that you do not recognize. Truth be told, it could save your marriage! Don't believe it? Here's proof.

Helen Fisher, a well-known sex and love researcher and anthropologist at Rutgers University, says, "based on MRI scans taken during that 'crazed, can't-think-of-anything-but' state of romance, that feeling is a biological drive to focus on one person.

There is increased blood flow to areas of the brain with a high number of dopamine receptors. Dopamine is associated with states of craving, euphoria, even addiction. In this early stage of a relationship, couples focus on each other to the exclusion of almost everything else.

Chemicals influence us biologically to act on our best behavior and to minimize flaws in the one we love. This is the *rush* or excitement felt early on. It is fun and passion-filled, but not exactly what to expect from the relationship down the road. Sooner or later, the body returns to a normal state as chemistry settles back into homeostasis (balance). When that happens and the realities and complexities of life return, the honeymoon stage of a relationship is usually over.

Going back to living in the real world can feel like a big letdown. Although this may sound like a gloom and doom attitude, the news is really not that bad! Your hormones don't desert you. Other neurochemicals, such as oxytocin and vassopressin, when released after orgasm and snuggling, can help a couple form and sustain a more lasting bond.

For years after meeting Terri I frequently thought of her and wondered how she could have been so "in love" with such a beast. I wondered if they were still together – or even if she was still alive. I had long ago left Houston and was living and practicing on the East Coast, but thoughts of Terri haunted me. Could I have better helped her to avoid an unhappy fate?

In the arena of love and relationships, there seem to be many things that cannot be explained or rationalized. Perhaps if individuals could take a detached look at relationships before agreeing to long term commitment, people like Terri or the unhappy husband and wife down the street from you, or maybe even YOU, would be saved a lot of heartache.

Terri was only the beginning. Over the years I've seen many individuals and couples for therapy – often due to their inherent desires to mend or fix relationship issues. Some come for help begrudgingly – feeling "forced" by their partner to participate. Many others approach therapy filled with hope that I might work some kind of magic to restore the fairy tale existence they experienced when their relationship was new. Clients often arrive alone – afraid to include their partner in an initial consultation or having a partner who refuses to be there. Sometimes people seek solace after a relationship has ended.

Introduction

Rather frequently, a client will reveal that his or her partner was always difficult; short tempered, demanding, verbally abusive, rude, etc. These unwelcome behaviors were a problem from the beginning of the relationship. For some truly mystifying reason (and this could be a whole book by itself), the client saw the red flags, but thought things would get better. It is amazing how many people believe that marriage is a cure-all for bad behavior!

Every First Appointment

I gather historical information about each client, including parents' marriages, dating history, and how they've arrived at the decision that their current person is "the one." In almost every instance, the red flags that surface early in the relationship are alarming. Most conflicts revolve around basic approaches to daily life issues that two people contemplating marriage need to discuss before taking the plunge.

In most instances, groundwork for disagreement is laid during early stages of the courtship. It is bewildering that people quite simply overlook or ignore many obvious problems. The "love conquers all" mentality seems to be very pervasive. Many people hope and expect that marriage will fix day to day problems, and some actually believe that marriage will eventually sway their partner to see things their way. Too many of us make an unconscious decision to ignore red flags, because being in love feels so good, we simply don't want to ruin the moment.

Be very careful! My wish for this book is to help readers avoid the common, painful pitfalls and costly mistakes that come from entering a love commitment with eyes dangerously closed. Learn the **Seven Essential Conversations** to save yourself years of wasted time and heartache! The lessons discussed here can help you make the best possible match for yourself, and enter (or continue) your committed love relationship with eyes wide open.

> *"After the chills and fever of love,*
> *how nice is the 98.6 of marriage!"*
> *Mignon McLaughlin*

For a trained therapist – or even a casual observer, Terri's situation seems clear; and yet, when one is in the forest, it can be very hard to see the trees. If only more couples would enter therapy *before* getting married, to make sure they are able to work through their differences. Daily stresses and challenges are sure to arise in any marriage. It helps to be prepared!

Couples swept away by early feelings of love often refuse to consider the idea that their relationship might not always be loving. "Ignorance is bliss." However, to remain ignorant and unable to see fault lines in a relationship is *not* a healthy way to enter marriage. Differences don't necessarily mean that a couple shouldn't be together, but they do need to be openly and specifically discussed, so that typical life situations don't harm the relationship's success down the road.

Having these discussions about your marriage helps both partners acknowledge the seriousness of the undertaking. It helps confirm that you are both looking ahead to the long, healthy, happy life you will build together. Investing time and energy to forge certain understandings now will ease or even eliminate typical difficulties in the future. You will surely disagree and may sometimes argue, but if from the very beginning of your life together you lay a foundation for listening to each other and create room for discussion, you will have the skills needed to tolerate differences and weather the inevitable storms.

Big Questions in Life

There are many questions to ask and answer when building a foundation for a life together. It's important to find out where your partner stands on money, sex, gender-roles, politics, religion and family. It's equally important to uncover where he or she stands on smaller things, like doing dishes or taking out the trash. Learning early on how your significant other feels about the large and mundane aspects of life will greatly increase your chances of being satisfied and happy with your decision to marry.

One problem may be that we have a hard time asking certain questions of ourselves. What do we want a mate to do for us? How can we communicate clearly before we determine what we want in a relationship?

> *"Love at first sight is easy to understand;*
> *it's when two people have been looking at each other for a lifetime*
> *that it becomes a miracle..."*
> *Amy Bloom*

What is it about being in love that causes otherwise intelligent, rational people to take huge leaps of faith without much evidence to support their decisions? I'm convinced that love is truly blind. Why else would rational people act so irrationally – even in the face of statistics showing that close to half of all marriages end in divorce? WHAT WERE THEY THINKING?

Right Brain/Left Brain

Many scientists have studied the phenomena of our two brain hemispheres and how they work very independently from each other. The left-brain is the organized, linear, efficient "get things done" side. The day to day processes of navigating life occur in the left-brain. We negotiate the ins and outs of our shared existence using left-brain tools.

The right-brain, on the other hand, is more abstract. It's the artistic, creative, non-linear side. Emotions are a function of the right-brain; we fall in love with the right-brain.

The corpus callosum is the chasm between the separated right and left cerebral hemispheres. Men have a wider area to bridge and less connecting tissue than women. This may be why men tend to experience things either rationally (left) or emotionally (right), but rarely both at the same time. As a result, the two hemispheres don't communicate very well with each other. This just might explain a huge problem in relationships.

To further complicate communication, men and women are inherently different. Biological variations between males and females go deeper than the obvious. Researchers at the University of Pittsburgh Medical School are finding that "sex-based disparities in the nervous, musculoskeletal, respiratory, cardio-vascular, and immune systems" exist.

According to Elaine Vitone, writing in the Fall 2010 Edition of *Pitt Med,* "They're finding strengths and vulnerabilities in each sex that further our understanding of certain illnesses overall." This has consequences in every aspect of life, from how the sexes approach problem-solving, to stress responses, to basic communication.

It is a common perception that women are more emotionally open, intuitive and connected, while men are more logical and less emotionally aware. This perception has a basis in biology as well as culture. Looking again at neurochemistry, Dr. Roger Sperry discovered a difference in the way male and female babies develop. Sometime between the 16th and 26th week of pregnancy, a chemical bath of testosterone is released in the brains of male babies and estrogen in female babies, leading to very different "hard wiring."

These chemicals naturally slow the development of the right hemisphere, the seat of intuition and empathy, the source of emotion. Though men have larger brains and more brain cells, women have more neural connections, so when a woman brings up something emotional that happened in the past during a current argument, that's because for her, the same emotion from past and present are connected.

Because women can access both sides of their brains more easily than men, female language is often formed from both hemispheres, whereas male language is more often based in the left hemisphere. This is one reason why women who have left-brain strokes have (on average) an easier time recovering language skills than men.

The inferior-parietal lobe (IPL), in the left hemisphere, is thought to be the seat of mathematical ability. Men typically develop a larger IPL than women, which explains why men often outperform women in math. Men also generally have stronger spacial abilities, whereas a thicker parietal area in women's brains is thought to hinder their ability to imagine 3D objects. Einstein, on the other hand, had an IPL that was not only larger than average, but also uniquely formed.

Men and women generally react differently to stress. According to psychologist Shelley E. Taylor, women "tend and befriend" stress. During times of stress, the body produces more of the hormone oxytocin. In women, estrogen enhances the effects of oxytocin, producing a calming effect, causing women to take better care of themselves and their children, and to seek out and strengthen bonds of friendship.

In men, stress increases levels of testosterone, and this reduces the stress-mitigating effects of oxytocin. This can cause men to withdraw, to think things through on their own. These physiological facts are another example of differences between males and females that make them approach problem-solving and communication differently.

Cultural learning adds an additional gendered layer. Women are raised to be sensitive to the emotions of others, while men are taught to act assertively to get what they want. The full weight of western culture has decided that reason is more important than emotion, without much thought given to finding an essential balance. As a result, men are raised to repress their feelings, while women are taught that their emotions are irrelevant.

As they grow, men are encouraged to disconnect from experiences of sadness and pain by not overtly reacting to them. Women are socialized to repress the expression of their thoughts and opinions, and avoid confrontation. Uncomfortable with and socialized away from overt demands, they often make requests which men may interpret as optional. In some cases men might see such requests as manipulative. Because being direct is often considered unfeminine, women are in a classic double bind. If they are assertive, they may be considered mannish, but if unassertive, they may be seen as frivolous or worse, as having no desires at all.

Women, with their greater volume of neural connections, remember things better than men. Unfortunately, in an argument, women tend to bring up everything related to the issue at hand, because, in their mind, it's all connected. To a man, this can feel like his partner is throwing the kitchen sink at him. All of these communication challenges factor into potential relationship problems.

I'm sure by now you may be thinking, "Then it's hopeless. How can I trust my experiences?" Well, the good news is that it is not hopeless. In fact, if you understand these principles and fundamental differences between men and women, and how to work through them, you have a much greater chance for a loving relationship that will last a lifetime.

Once you recognize that the early highs of a relationship are not sustainable over the long term, it's important to make sure there is substance that can carry your love beyond those early feelings, to stand the test of time. The underpinnings of a healthy relationship (which we will discuss in depth in the chapters to follow) are often overlooked, but they are where the substance is – much like a bridge that seems to float over the water, but is solidly supported underneath. When it comes to living a lifetime with another, there must be more to support and justify the relationship than simply feelings of love.

Your Communication Toolkit

It's important to create a physically and emotionally neutral space where conversation can take place. Strive to establish an open, safe, comfortable haven within which to share feelings, thoughts, fears and dreams for the future. This helps both partners feel safe initiating a conversation about anything. Anything can be said if it is said with compassion and integrity; with respect for the dignity of your partner. Talking together is about more than just the words you say to each other. It's also how you say them (ie: non-verbal communications such as facial expression and body language).

A lot also depends on how you are heard. Listening with your whole self is crucial to effective communication. Listen to the words, but also the intentions behind the words. Notice the emotions underneath what your partner is saying; look for non-verbal cues. Try to focus on the present and listen fully, without judgment, without working mentally on what you will say in return, and without comparing what your partner is saying to previous statements. Above all, keep an open mind and avoid instant reactions. Listening is the most powerful and sincere way of showing your partner you care.

It is essential to learn to communicate with your partner without placing blame. Lack of fear of judgment creates the connection and trust for true communication to happen. Remember that it is human nature to retreat or become defensive when one feels blamed. When we feel we are being attacked, we stop listening. We start to think of all the things we disagree with, and prepare to respond with further blame. Does this sound familiar? No problem can be solved this way.

If you truly want to establish good communication and work together to solve problems, you must give up your attachment to being right. Be sure to voice appreciation about your partner much more often than you complain. Accentuating the positive makes it easier to work out the inevitable kinks. If you're bothered by your partner's communication style, try to pinpoint what the issue is. Take time to make sure that your exchanges are productive.

If you don't agree with your partner, don't interrupt. It is especially when you disagree that you must listen most closely, without judgment, and without becoming defensive. Don't simply think about what you will say when it's, 'your turn'. That's disrespectful and counter-productive. Even if you are dead sure that you're right (and sometimes you will be, but sometimes you won't), ask yourself, would you rather be right, or happy?

Every relationship depends upon two different people who are bound to have different opinions. Remember that differences add spice to life. Try to be accepting. If you're unsure about what your partner means, paraphrase your understanding of what you heard, and ask if your interpretation is correct. If not, ask for further clarification. Take a minute to compose yourself if you are flustered or angry.

Clarity is key to good communication. Women tend to be more indirect, but a direct and clear request for what you want will be better heard by men. An example of being indirect: a woman might object to an idea but express this objection by asking questions. In the absence of a direct objection, your man, not schooled in picking up nonverbal cues, might tend to ignore or discount these questions. On the other hand, women also ask questions simply to gather information, just as men do. If you are willing to compromise, then do so. Be prepared to negotiate for what you want; marriage is a give and take situation. If you cook dinner, ask your partner if he/she will clean up afterwards.

Both left and right-brain states bring important skills to communicating and problem solving with compassion. Strive to develop a balance between these hemispheric qualities. When your communication comes from love and respect, you're on the right path.

Men and women use conversation in different ways. While women use 'small talk' to build rapport, discussing relationships and personal experiences comfortably - men tend to view conversation as little more than a way to exchange information or work on a problem.

Introduction

"Love: A temporary insanity, curable by marriage."
Ambrose Bierce

In order to ensure that your left-brain is able to go along
with the program your right-brain has plunged you into, it
is important for any couple to sit down and have some crucial
left-brain conversations. Discuss the practical issues of creating
a successful and fulfilling life together.

You see, while love is important, it takes more than love to
make a relationship work. Many couples tend to fall in love
and overlook the needs of the left-brain. Others may actually
be or stay together for practical "it makes good sense" reasons,
without any intense emotional connection at all.

While this book primarily addresses the majority of couples
who are led into a relationship by their right-brain, it can
happen in reverse. Either way, my premise is that *both the
right-brain and the left-brain must be satisfied for a relationship
to survive and thrive.* After the extraordinary right-brain joy of
falling in love, you'll need to cultivate the everyday left-brain
happiness of building a lasting marriage.

The following chapters are a guide to *seven essential conversations* worth having before marriage. Consider this guided
list an opportunity to embark on a quest together, for deeper
knowledge of each other. You're on a journey toward even
greater intimacy, as two minds begin the work of sharing a life.
Your time together will be strengthened by authenticity and
defenselessness, for it is truly courageous to love another with
your whole being. This is the life blood, the sap of marriage that

will keep it evergreen. When couples can navigate this, there is a very good possibility of divorce proofing the relationship before saying "I do."

There is no right or wrong answer to how you, as a couple, should handle the issues that are raised in this book. The important thing is that you agree on a plan that will work for both of you. You don't have to be in lockstep with each other, either. It is fine to have differing opinions. Face it, if you were each the other's clone, life would be very boring, indeed.

What matters most is your ability to a) respect your partner's differences, and b) find ways to deal with them. Marriage is often more about agreeing to disagree, than about agreeing on everything. When you can remain respectful of each other's choices without resentment, you're headed for success. After all, a relationship does not blend two people into one. The goal is not to think alike, but to think together.

How to Use this Book

I suggest taking one chapter at a time. Read it together and discuss the issues that it raises. Put yourself in hypothetical situations to anticipate how you would address them as a couple, should they arise in your life together. As you read the brief case summaries, see which ones mimic your relationship and which partner most closely resembles you or your partner.

When you reach the end of each chapter and get to the suggested list of questions for consideration, one idea is to each review the questions separately, on your own as individuals, first. "Know Thyself" is Rule Number One! You must really understand what you want and don't want in your relationship before you can expect to be able to adequately communicate those needs and desires to your partner.

Once you've both determined your wishes and concerns in private, come together and share what you've learned. As you fill in the blanks with your personal thoughts, ideas and feelings, you will quickly learn a lot about yourself, and your partner. We've all heard many times that knowledge is power, so here's to you and a powerfully successful relationship in your future.

"One of the first things a relationship therapist learns is that couples burn up energy that should be used for something else. In fact, arguments often serve the purpose of using up energy so the couple doesn't have to take the courageous, creative leap into an unknown fear. Arguing serves the function of being a zone of familiarity into which you can retreat when you are making a creative breakthrough."
Gay Hendricks

Chapter One

Personal Habits, Preferences and Idiosyncrasies

"I love being married. It's so great to find that one special person you want to annoy for the rest of your life."
Rita Rudner

Each of us is our own unique person. This is as it should be. Sometimes our idiosyncrasies can be charming, sometimes annoying. Unfortunately, the traits that we once found charming early in a relationship can become annoying over time.

Some personal preferences involve significant lifestyle terms that leave little room for compromise. Most people notice fairly quickly the little habits lovers have that constantly irritate. The longer two people are together, the more obvious tiny habits will seem.

I've heard many spouses claim that they believe their partner continues to engage in certain habits purely out of spite. The truth is that many of the little things that make each of us unique as individuals are deeply embedded into our behavior.

Too many people enter marriage thinking that they will be able to change their mate over time. This is a significant and dangerous misconception that must be given serious thought prior to entering a life-long commitment. It's pretty safe to assume that during the dating period, you are only seeing your new love interest at his/her very best!

"What you are as a single person, you will be as a married person, only to a greater degree. Any negative character trait will be intensified in a marriage because you will feel free to let your guard down...."

Josh McDowell

Tim & Linda's Story

Tim and Linda were best friends. They had similar views about many important things in life. They were each quite independent and gave one another the space they needed to flourish as free spirits. They respected each other's opinions, shared common interests and friends, and generally got along famously. In fact, Tim and Linda might have easily sailed through all of the discussions mentioned in this book.

There was, however, one thing that seemed so tiny, at least initially. Linda was a morning person. She usually hit the ground running at 6 AM, loving the quiet of early morning hours when she could do her yoga before the phone started to ring and the day grew hectic. By 10 PM, Linda was winding down and getting ready for bed, having put in a very full day. Tim, on the other hand, was a night person. On work days, he would drag himself out of bed at 8AM and not be fully awake until after his third cup of coffee.

On weekends, Tim could easily sleep until noon. Then, he'd be ready for a night on the town. Linda would try to hang in there with him when they went out, but often ended up feeling like a "party pooper" when she was ready to go home before midnight. She knew her body would have her wide awake again at 6AM – weekend or not. Linda often wished on weekends that Tim would get up and share the peaceful joys of morning with her.

At first, this seemed like a harmless difference; but over time a difference like this can become wearing. In Tim and Linda's case, it left them little time to actually be together as husband and wife. Neither partner was wrong or right, but such vast differences in personal routine and lifestyle can wreak havoc on a marriage. It's difficult to find a balance that doesn't compromise one person over the other, leaving a negative impact after any change.

Fortunately, because Tim and Linda were such independent people, they determined that they could be fine giving each other space to be themselves. When their therapist reframed the situation as giving them each an opportunity for "personal time," their differences became more acceptable and even desirable.

When going out for the evening, especially if it was a party, they would either take separate cars, or one would catch a ride home with a friend. This would not work for everyone, but it was the perfect solution for Tim and Linda.

Another couple both loved music – but not the same kind. She was a classical music buff and he liked heavy metal. When they were both home, the sound system was silent, because the other's music was like fingernails on a chalkboard. Naturally it was impossible for them to find LIVE music they could agree to attend together. As a result, they never went out to hear live music together – and this was genuinely missed, because it had once been a favorite activity that they each enjoyed with friends.

Couples can disagree on leisure activities, taste in food, movies, vacations, etc. Some have differences in personal or household hygiene and what degree of cleanliness is sufficient. One person might skip a shower on a Saturday or let dishes soak in the sink overnight. The other person might find that disgusting.

Some people exhibit excessive, over-the-top behaviors or addic-tions that inevitably harm them and their relationships. Very driven Type A personalities may be focused, hard-working and financially successful, but become so invested in their career, that their relationships suffer. Where do you stand on this? Are you a workaholic? Or do you take time for pleasure, making sure to stop and smell the roses?

There are people who are critical, while others are validating and affirming. Some have a great sense of humor (or at least, THEY think they're funny), while others are serious.

None of these characteristics are necessarily deal-breakers. There is almost always room for compromise, and yet relationship success often boils down to compatibility. The key is to recognize the differences between you early, and agree on ways to deal with those differences *before* you make a life-long commitment. When you choose to ignore warning signs or small conflicts and push them under the rug during the early days of your relationship, you are only setting yourself and your partner up for disappointment and heartache later on.

> *"It destroys one's nerves*
> *to be amiable every day to the same person."*
> Benjamin Disraeli

Marian & Chip's Story

Marian and Chip have been married for seven years. They know each others' idiosyncrasies all too well. There are two basic issues that Marian and Chip can't seem to agree on. The first is house cleaning and the second is sleeping arrangements.

Marian is definitely a Type A personality. She cleans some part of the house every day, picks up after herself and thoroughly expects things to remain clean. When she goes about tidying a room, she does the whole thing from top to bottom until it's spotless. Light, surface cleaning is not in Marian's repertoire.

Chip is more of a 'throw everything under the bed' kind of guy. As long as things look neat and picked-up, that is clean enough for him. Although both do their share around their home, the disagreements come from who is doing it properly. Chip accuses Marian of being anal, and Marian accuses Chip of being haphazard.

Marian gets so disgusted with Chip's house cleaning that she ends up redoing everything he does. Chip then decides that there's little reason to try, since Marian will redo his work anyhow. The struggle here is that these two people have entirely different ideas and methods of house cleaning. Working toward some kind of balance is clearly necessary.

The second disagreement between Chip and Marian is the fact that Chip snores...loudly! After many years of plopping on the couch, Marian is frustrated and angry that Chip won't do something about his snoring. She feels that he is intentionally trying to annoy her. Because Marian won't sleep in the same room with him, Chip feels that this affects their intimacy.

Both the house cleaning and snoring were obvious issues before they got married. Marian saw Chip's apartment while they dated and knew that he was a slob. She was also aware of the fact that he snored so loudly, it sometimes woke the neighbors. These issues, although seemingly small, often loom large and may even become grounds for divorce.

When one person refuses to change for the other, their continued behavior is seen as a lack of love or respect. In some cases this may be accurate. In others, it may be totally unfair to expect change in the first place. In Marian and Chip's case, they sought counseling and came to a compromise that seems to be working. Every evening before dinner, Chip spends 15 or 20 minutes straightening up his messes so they never get over-whelming.

Messing with someone's ability to sleep through the night can have potential for pretty serious long-term damage. Getting a consistently good night's sleep is important for everyone, and we start to resent it when we don't get the sleep we need. Chip was fitted with a night guard by his dentist, and this has helped his snoring immensely. But there are many other potential con-flicts besides house cleaning and snoring.

Do you like to cuddle close in a small bed or spread out in a King-size? How long does it take you to drift off and how easily do you awaken in the night? Perhaps you have different inter-nal thermostats and one of you is perpetually cold while the other is sweating. Maybe one of you likes to read before sleep, while the other must fall asleep with the TV on. These days, many bedrooms have become another recreation room; with TVs, games, computers and cell phones. People often think that the time just before bed is a found hour to get just a little extra work done.

Ideally, to cultivate good sleep habits that give you consistent rest, take the advice of sleep experts and use your bedroom only for sleeping or sex. Let it be a private haven that promotes peace and calm in an otherwise chaotic world. TV and other distractions bring a lot of outside stimulation, sometimes so much that it disrupts sleep. Having the TV on can wake you frequently and fragment your sleep throughout the night.

If you can't agree on sleep protocols or other minor grievances, at least be aware of your respective preferences, which is the first step to compromise. Talk through your differences and try to find a happy medium.

If the problem truly is snoring, you can consult a specialist to make sure there is no underlying problem or sleep apnea. Sometimes snoring can be minimized by sleeping in a special posture, but sometimes it can't be resolved in a way that works for both partners. In the end, it may be necessary to consider separate bedrooms. Believe it or not, this is more common than you may think, and it doesn't have to mean disaster for your relationship. You can still visit, snuggle and have sex any time, but you also have a sanctuary retreat for when your partner turns into a chainsaw.

Do you habitually avoid chores or other duties in your marriage? If this comes up, at least acknowledge that you've heard what your partner's said. Even when you don't agree, or don't want to change, it's respectful to let someone you care about know that they've been heard.

It's equally important to offer support and positive reinforcement when your partner is making a concerted effort to change an entrenched habit. Whether a loved one is working on weight loss, trying to quit smoking, or something similarly challenging, try to be understanding. It takes a while to instill a new habit or break an old one, but it can be done!

Zack & Elise's Story

Before children came, Zack and Elise were both busy workaholics, equally obsessed with their careers. If Zack stayed late at the office, this suited Elise just fine, because nine times out of ten she was working late too. They got along fine when it was just the two of them; eating take-out most nights, going to an event at the last minute because their schedules freed up, and cramming in extra work at home on the weekends. Because they both enjoyed their jobs, Zack and Elise each understood the importance of letting the other have time needed to accomplish certain projects or take advantage of new opportunities.

When children came along, however, the picture quickly changed. Elise decided she would rather cut back on work to be a more attentive mom to their children. She enjoyed many aspects of parenting and homemaking that had never interested her before. The one thing she found increasingly irksome, was Zack's workaholic tendencies. They kept him away from the family many nights and many weekends. She had changed. He had not.

Elise tried to accommodate Zack's schedule, holding dinner until the time Zack said he'd be home. The problem was, Zack often didn't come home when he said he would, and Elise would be waiting with an elaborate dinner, feeling neglected and foolish. Worse, she'd sometimes worry that something terrible had happened to him. When he would finally come home late and tired, Elise would accost him angrily for not having called. Naturally, Zack would become defensive and an argument ensued.

While Elise would have ideally liked Zack to come home at dinner time, the compromise they reached was reasonable: dinner would be served at a specific time and he would call if he was going to be late. If he was going to be late, he was going to heat leftovers and would miss quality time with his kids. The family wouldn't continue to hold up their routines for Zack's long hours.

If you find yourself criticizing your partner often, or feel like you're always on the defensive, this is a red flag. PAY ATTENTION. The more you withdraw from each other without trying to resolve your differences, the larger that task will loom. Communicating well is a skill that needs to be practiced.

Getting back to gender differences, John Gray in *Men are From Mars, Women are From Venus,* talks about the different rhythms of intimacy for men and women. "Men," Gray says, "are like rubber bands; and sometimes, for their own reasons, they need to retreat from intimacy and spend time alone. Sometimes that means zoning out in front of the TV. That's the wrong time to try to have a meaningful dialogue."

According to Gray, women are like waves in that they can be warm, generous and loving much of the time, but also have down days when the wave of love seems to retreat. Women feel emotionally depleted and especially vulnerable during this part of their intimacy cycle. It's often hard for men to pick up signals, and women can't always verbalize a specific problem that is haunting them.

It's easier on both parties if moods can be communicated openly. If you need to spend some time alone, assure your partner that you'll be back. When you take time out to think things through or unwind, make sure your mate knows that's all it is, so he doesn't have to wonder if you're retreating from them because you're upset.

If you need someone to simply listen when you're upset, without trying to solve the problem for you, then SAY so. You have a much better chance of getting what you need from your partner when you articulate it.

> *"If there's something you want,*
> *if there's something you need,*
> *you gotta raise your hand."*
> *Bruce Springsteen*

Take a <u>realistic</u> look at your partnership. Discover the little things that set you and your partner apart. Imagine yourself living the rest of your life with this person and their traits. What do you appreciate most? What can you easily accept, and what will drive you crazy? What, if any, are your "deal-breakers"?

Sometimes simple things are what drive couples apart, in the end. Pay attention as you review the following questions, to make sure that you're with the best mate for the lifestyle you want, or identify areas that you may need to work on.

Questions about Personal Habits, Preferences & Idiosyncrasies

1. Think about your partner. What is it about him/her that drives you nuts? Do you think these personal issues will change over time? If not, consider the long-term effects of living with these little 'habits.'

2. Discuss with each other your personal annoyances and try to form a contract for compromise in dealing with them. Determine what you each see as a road block and honestly reveal *why* these annoyances cause so much frustration.

3. Make a list of the little things that could be deal-breakers for you and discuss why.

4. What are the BIGGEST issues – maybe not in terms of life importance, but in terms of annoyance? Of the differences between you, decide which ones need to be worked on vs. which can be tolerated and left alone. Agree to disagree on at least a few!

"Love is blind; but marriage restores its sight!"
Georg Lichtenberg

Chapter Two

Money

Love may be blind, but marriage is a financial partnership as much as a romantic one, and it's best to enter it with eyes wide open. It's easy to neglect discussion of finances in favor of talking about wedding details. Some people fear that talking about money will spoil the glow of love, but that glow won't keep monthly bills from coming, or get you any closer to living in your dream house. Making dreams come true takes some forethought and common sense, so you'll need to focus an essential conversation on money.

If you dread talking money with your honey, you're not alone. Money is most often cited as a factor in divorce. It is the number one area of disagreement between spouses. Compounding the issue is that most of us (especially women) have been taught that it's impolite to talk about money. While that might be true at cocktail parties, it is a crucial subject to address with your partner before marriage.

Gone are the days when people married right out of high school or college. It used to be that the woman immediately became pregnant and spent her next 20 years as wife and homemaker, staying home with children while the husband went out into the world as exclusive breadwinner for the family. Today, most men and women wait until at least their late 20's to marry. Both partners have considerable work experience; meaning experience with earning – and spending – their own money. Neither is likely to be happy about giving up all their financial independence.

Even when one spouse later chooses to cut back or stop working to be an at-home parent for the children, they usually have the previous experience of financial autonomy.

Money can also be a tremendous source of self-esteem and power that many couples end up using as a stage upon which to act out deeper issues. The way we feel about money, how it's earned, spent or saved, the emotional issues it comes with, and the way it is (or isn't) valued and treated, are all important factors in a marriage.

While many people assume that financial matters are very straightforward, logical and "left-brained," nothing could be farther from the truth. People's attitudes about money are shaped by their upbringing, education, experiences, and even religion. Money is often attached to core beliefs about self-worth. It colors major life decisions, from relationships to career choices to how we spend our time.

Keeping silent about the emotions and assumptions that you associate with money doesn't mean they don't exist. If you don't talk about financial matters, hopes and challenges now, your respective assumptions will certainly come up at a later date; chances are in a less-than friendly way. Before combining your money with another person's, examine your own attitudes, needs and limitations carefully.

For example, one of the most prevalent thoughts about money is "Time is Money." Truly, money can save time when you're talking about remodeling your home. Money pays for expertise, which translates into time saved. However, people with this attitude about money often tend to equate affection with money, and substitute money for time spent together. For instance, a busy executive might buy his children lots of toys to substitute for the time he doesn't spend with them. This attitude can foster a belief that no other form of approval means as much as monetary approval, and that financial success is the only kind of success that matters.

Some people believe that "money is the root of all evil," that money, in fact, causes evil, because it has the power to corrupt. Do you ascribe such power to money? Look within and ask yourself which of your own values are incorruptible. You will likely find that you are deeply committed to your values and that whether or not you have a lot of money, they are durable.

For some people money is a necessary evil; something you exchange time for, because it pays the bills. For others, money is more valuable than any other pursuit in life because of what it means; whether that is freedom, power or success. Some feel that a financial portfolio is their "life's report card," the sole measure of their worth. For still others, money is a tool for personal growth, a means to an end. In some people, it can provoke feelings of being manipulated or owned. It can also be a symbol of vulgar excess.

It's important to understand your unconscious attitudes about money, because they may keep you from succeeding in love, and in life. Money and marriage are related in another way - many studies indicate that financial success fosters a happier marriage and a happy marriage contributes to financial success. On the other hand, when one partner feels dependent, inferior or cheated, financial disputes are bound to arise.

Much of the way we feel about having money or not having enough money is a result of our upbringing. This doesn't mean we can't compromise or change our attitudes, but it does mean that people approach a marital union with the financial baggage of personal and family history. Understanding your own feelings about money and comparing them with your partner's is crucial. Identify financial issues early and develop solutions you can both live with comfortably. This is fundamental to the success of any marriage.

Mary & John's Story

Mary and John are college graduates in their late 20's. They both hold down good jobs. After dating for a year, they recently became engaged. Mary and John came to my office because although they shared many important values, they were having big disagreements about money.

Mary came from a very frugal family. Her parents worked hard, saved their money, and never incurred any debt until they purchased a home. Even then, they bought a home that was very much within their means – simple, basic, and not a stretch in terms of the monthly payment. Mary's family rarely took a vacation and when they did, they stayed with family members.

Chapter Two: Money

Money was tight in this blue collar household, but Mary's parents always budgeted. They rarely used credit cards, so there were never interest charges or late fees. When they used credit cards, they were paid in full at the end of the month.

Quality always trumped quantity in Mary's household. When she would go shopping with her mother, her mother didn't look for what was cheapest, but rather, what was the best *value*. If she couldn't afford something that was well made and durable, she would go without – waiting until she could afford it – rather than buying something of inferior quality. When something was on sale that the family routinely used, such as paper products, Mary's mother would buy a case and store the box in the basement.

When Mary received money as a gift, she was taught to save it rather than go out and spend it on a toy she would soon outgrow. Mary's family had closely managed their money. They respected money and the effort it took to earn it, so they guarded it. Having substantial savings for the proverbial rainy day gave them a sense of security.

Mary came into her relationship with John debt-free and with substantial savings. When John suggested they shop for an engagement ring, she stated that she'd rather take that money and use it for a down payment on their first house.

John's family had a very different approach to money. They believed that money was to be spent and enjoyed. What was the purpose of hard work if you didn't have anything to show for it? John's family earned more money than Mary's and certainly had more "stuff" – a bigger house, all the latest gadgets, and huge credit card debt.

John's family took a two week vacation every year, and often went into debt to pay for it. They considered it their reward for a year of hard work, something they deserved and that the kids were entitled to – whether it broke the budget or not. John always spent the money his grandparents gave him for his birthday on special treats for himself – a new toy, or tickets to a concert. When they got engaged, John had an expensive new car (and new car loan), and about $ 15,000 in credit card debt.

Mary was concerned about John's spending and she wasn't comfortable investing her savings in a house for the two of them while John's money went to retire his debt (or maybe just maintain his spending). She rightly saw that this difference in spending habits was a prescription for resentment down the road.

The situation John and Mary faced is a common one. It isn't that either of them was "right" or "wrong." It could be argued that each was a bit extreme in their approach, but actually, these differences are quite common. The question was how to resolve their money issues in a way that would work for both of them. Both had respectable incomes, but vastly different ideas about how they should be spent. In order to find a mutual solution, we first made a list of necessary mutual expenses – rent, utilities, food, insurance, etc.

Mary and John agreed to put a specific amount of money, proportionate to their incomes, into a household checking account that would cover their common living expenses, plus a bit more to build up an emergency fund. They also put an agreed-upon amount into a money market fund each month, to save for a down payment on a house. This was a value and goal that they shared.

John and Mary kept individual checking accounts that were totally discretionary – each could spend from their account however they chose to. John's car payment came out of his account. Mary had paid cash for a small late model used car, so she was able to save some of her discretionary money for something she might want in the future. Clothing, gifts, and other incidentals were paid for out of these individual accounts.

This arrangement worked well for John and Mary. From time to time issues had to be negotiated – such as who would contribute how much to vacations – but they were able to reach acceptable compromises.

I think this method worked for Mary and John because it didn't require either of them to completely forego their way of doing things, so they didn't entirely lose their financial autonomy. The arrangement honored their desire to contribute in an equitable way to their life together.

Obviously, this particular setup might not work for everyone. Sometimes there is significant disparity in individual earnings. Sometimes, only one member of the couple earns an income. Different arrangements need to be worked out for different circumstances. What's important is that these issues are discussed and decided upon at the beginning of your life together.

Different couples come up with different money management systems. Traditionally, one partner, most often the wife, manages the household expenses. If the husband is the sole earner, he may give the wife an allowance to cover household finances, and how she manages that budget is up to her. The husband then keeps control over the rest of the money.

In another system, husband and wife pool their incomes into one account that both have equal access to. In some marriages, each spouse controls their own income with a set of rules or general understanding about who pays for what. Often, where the wife makes as much as or more than the husband, each partner manages their own income with a portion going into a combined account to cover household expenses. If incomes are similar, the expenses are usually shared evenly. When there is a large wage gap, it's wise to set a percentage of income to contribute. Separate accounts allow each partner to feel some autonomy in financial decisions, which is a good way to avoid petty arguments over who spends how much on incidentals and hobbies. Gift-giving is also easier and more of a surprise. Be sure to discuss what items constitute household expenses, so agreed contributions are clear and unnecessary conflicts are avoided. Monthly bills may be obvious, but it's important to also remember savings, investments and vacations.

To some extent, solving money issues can help to define roles within a marriage. Perhaps one person is a better investor and so should be the person in charge of investments. Beware though, that this kind of dynamic can be enabling: for a wife who wants a father figure to take care of her, or a man who will put money into an account managed by his wife, only to criticize her every decision.

Sometimes there are unspoken, perhaps even unconscious, expectations. It is best to be clear about assumptions: if your wife works to put you through medical school, then once you graduate she expects to quit her job and raise children. Or, if your husband covers the expenses alone while the children are young, he expects you to get a part-time job to help out with finances once the little ones are in school.

Life's circumstances are not stagnant. There is no doubt an ebb and flow that requires previous agreements to be modified. The key is to continue to make plans and subsequent adjustments that are true to the individual values of each partner, while also helping to support each other's needs.

Bob & Laura's Story

Bob and Laura had been married for just over a year. They both earned respectable incomes and worked hard. Upon their marriage they immediately combined all of their assets, bought a home and began using a single checking account for all the bills. Neither said much to the other in regard to how money was being spent or who did the spending. Bob left it to Laura to pay all the bills, which she did, happily. She would line the bills on the kitchen table and meticulously write checks to make sure their utilities, car payments and necessities were paid for.

Bob had little if any interest in actually looking at the bills. He felt that as long as they were being paid on time, it didn't matter how much they came to. What soon happened, however, is that Bob would use money from their joint account as a discretionary fund, buying parts for his motorcycle or splurging on gifts for Laura with no accurate idea of how much money was actually available to spend.

When Laura would confront Bob, he was indignant, feeling that since he made a decent income he should be able to spend it without asking. Laura felt that her discretionary money for new clothes or the hair salon was being limited because she *was* acutely aware of the bills. She soon found that by the end of each month, she was forced to stretch their income to an uncomfortable degree.

Sometimes Bob would randomly make large purchases without talking to Laura. When those bills came in, it was especially difficult to pay on top of the usual budget. Bob couldn't believe that with two incomes and no kids there were actually weeks that were tight. He accused Laura of spending all the money. Laura defended herself by saying that she was spending all the money, but it was on the household bills.

This came to a volcanic head one day when Bob used a bonus check to buy himself another motorcycle, and Laura, trying to get ahead, had written several checks for the next month's car and mortgage payments. Needless to say, when the checks started bouncing, they were bouncing into my office.

Chapter Two: Money

In this situation, as is often the case, neither partner is right or wrong. However, it's clear that Bob and Laura made a hasty decision to combine incomes without talking about how money should be dispersed, or building a realistic budget for routine bills. Laura knew what was due, so she was forced to cut back on things that were important to her, while Bob was spending money as freely as before their marriage. Laura began to feel resentful, throwing bills on the table so that Bob could take over the household finances. Bob retaliated by letting them sit there, going unpaid. He felt deprived, angered, limited and controlled by his new wife.

This conflict was quite simply a lack of communication. Before they were married, Bob and Laura had each paid their own way (living separately) and used their excess funds to spend or save as they liked. Once married, Bob took comfort from knowing that Laura would handle everything, while Laura was left with the responsibilities and burdens of managing their household budget.

Since Bob's spending was unpredictable and often significant, Laura was forced to confront Bob about where money was going. This caused Bob to feel controlled. Neither partner wanted to give up their autonomy, yet neither of them felt safe talking about the situation. The solution was to set up a household account that they contributed to equally for bills. Then, each of them opened their own savings or discretionary spending account. In addition, they sat down twice a month to review incoming and outgoing bills, so that both of them had an accurate picture of the household's financial responsibilities and balances. This allowed Bob and Laura to adjust their joint account contributions and personal spending as needed.

If each spouse earns approximately the same income and you each have approximately the same amount of debt, you can start your financial life together on a fairly level playing field. This field can get muddy when children come along if one parent needs to spend more time at home, meaning less time earning. When children are born, spending needs to be altered and a new plan needs to be devised.

A large wage gap between spouses can be an issue. It is vitally important to craft solutions that manage to stay flexible as life situations change. Be mindful that at some point one partner may lose their job or be forced to take a painful pay cut. The reality is that medical expenses or other unforeseen situations are likely to arise during the course of a marriage.

If this is a second marriage for either or both of you, money matters may be even more complicated. The need to factor in alimonies, child support payments and previous debt make the finance conversation even more essential. When money decisions involve children, try to include them in the discussions. When children are a part of deciding budget priorities, they are more likely to stick with and respect decisions made. It's important for young people to understand the value of resisting an impulse to buy, in favor of saving for larger wishes and items truly desired.

Chapter Two: Money

Who earns more money can easily change over the years, but the one who contributes more to the household fund has greater power within the marriage. For this reason, it's important to decide together early on how money policies will be decided, regardless of who earns the most. Determine the big money decisions for your shared future: buying a home, sending your children to college, etc. It's good to also define smaller purchases that can be decided autonomously, like items for the home not exceeding $200.

A dilemma sometimes arises for couples when it comes to accepting help or gifts from family. The help might be money for a down payment on the house of your dreams, but strings attached to gifts from parents or in-laws can sometimes be a way to exercise control through purse strings. Consider obligations that may come with monetary support. Will the generous family member then decide it's okay to stop by anytime, unannounced?

What will be the consequences if, at some point in the future, you and the family member don't see eye to eye? The family member may want to pay to send your child to a good private school that emphasizes a particular religion. This can pose conflict if you yourself are of a different faith. These potential difficulties need to be out in the open before you focus on linens and flowers for a wedding reception.

Gift-giving within marriage is an expression of love and the give-and-take of your intimate relationship. Ideally, gifts should be judged by their value and thoughtfulness, not their price, but discussing financial parameters keeps exchanges fair.

Finding answers to money problems takes a lot of forethought and honesty. We all have to know what we are willing to give up, and what we are not willing to do without. Answers to this will change over the course of a lifetime, so maintaining clear and open dialogue will help both partners take responsibility for decision making. Shared ownership of financial decisions is vital. When one partner feels entitled to his or her way over the other, resentment will fester. Let it be a comfort to know that there are a wide range of solutions that will work for different couples, depending upon each financial situation.

Talking about money gives couples the opportunity to discuss and set long-term life goals together, then map out a way to achieve them. Setting financial goals is a crucial first step to meeting them. Studies show that those who take the time to write down their goals, are often the most successful in achieving them.

When setting goals, remember the obvious: they will not be achieved all at once. If you're in debt, remember that it took you years to dig yourself in and it will take some time to dig yourself out. It can be frustrating, but try to separate your emotions from the facts.

Your life together doesn't have to be run like a business, but there are business techniques that serve marriage well. A family, for all else that it is, is a small economic unit with income and expenses. As such, certain business fundamentals apply. For example, you can have an agreed upon budget with regular reviews. You might do research and have discussions before any major purchases.

EXERCISE: Write each financial goal on an index card. Be specific. What is the desired wish? What will it cost? When would you like to reach this goal? Sort cards into short-term (what you hope/expect to accomplish within 1 to 5 years) and long-term goals. Go through all the piles together and prioritize them. Next, divide the cost of each goal by the number of months it will take to achieve it (the number of years multiplied by 12). This will tell you the amount you need to save to accomplish your goal. If it's more than you can set aside each month, rethink the importance of this goal. Can you adjust the timeline? Would you be willing to get a second job to make it happen? Will you sacrifice in other spending areas to help this wish come true?

Set aside allowances. What can either partner spend, 'no questions asked'? This gives both partners a reasonable amount of financial autonomy, and averts arguments over buying personal items. If any one area of spending seems excessive, be sure to discuss it. Keep careful track of all expenses and, if necessary, adjust spending to be more in line with your overall budget.

Speaking of budget, you might as well make one now. Virtually every book about money management recommends setting up a budget to follow, which includes not only your expenses, but savings. Gail Vaz-Oxlade, in her book *Debt-Free Forever*, talks about the "Life Pie," where she suggests that the percentage you spend on your housing should not exceed 35% of your income and savings should make up at least 10% of your income, with debt no greater than 15%. Keep in mind when setting a budget that you cannot spend more than you make without going into debt. If you're in debt, you'll never get out of it making minimum payments. You must pay more than the minimum to make progress.

Men and women generally agree on the ten highest financial priorities; with rent, mortgage, food and medical insurance topping the list. Disagreements between couples often begin over how to spend disposable income or unexpected windfalls.

Discussing bills and making financial decisions should be a part of your monthly routine. Set aside a time and place, free from distractions. If children will be affected by money decisions, include them in these discussions. It's easier for them to understand limits and goals when they are involved in the process. Encourage free expression of wants, desires and opinions. Keep accurate, up-to-date financial records to maintain objectivity.

Once a year, perhaps right after the New Year begins, when you're starting to look at taxes, you and your partner need to have a more in-depth conversation about finances. It's important for you to both thoroughly understand your financial situation and have a plan in place in case of an emergency.

Do you both know where to find important documents like past tax returns, investment information, wills and insurance documents? Do you have an accurate balance sheet that details your debts and assets? It's important to make time to reassess your budget, add any new considerations and look ahead for the coming year.

Take a look at how you've agreed to pay bills and whether or not this system is still working for both of you. Take time to reflect on your progress toward previously established financial goals. If there are areas of obvious vulnerability in your financial picture, talk it out and see what you might be able to do about it. Think about how you can strengthen your financial health.

The beginning of a relationship is the best time to talk about money, but it's never too late to make this essential conversation a part of your routine. It should be a relaxed discussion rather than a reaction to financial crisis, so the more ordinary the timing, the better.

If you are planning to get married, be sure to take a look at the following questions about money. First, each of you read them separately. Write down your answers privately, so that you can consider them on your own first, void of conversation and debate. After you've both done this, come together and compare your answers.

It is just as important to discuss options, choices and reasons for making each choice, as it is to simply share your answers. Each of you will gain a better understanding of the other's point of view. Go over difficult questions again – those where you have disagreement - and discuss any compromising response that would be suitable to both of you. Keep in mind that when it comes to money, you must leave room for flexibility.

If you aren't comfortable with your partner's financial values, you need to figure out why. Perhaps you've always been financially independent and you find the idea of having to discuss every expenditure objectionable. Perhaps you're starting out with a greater net worth and you worry about your partner's

spending habits. If you can't sort out your financial disagreements by following these guidelines, consider seeking the help
of a financial consultant or therapist.

"Our marriage has always been a 50-50 proposition, with the
possible exception of closet space..."
Gene Perret -1968

Questions to Discuss about Money

1. How do you feel about the way your parents handled money in your childhood home? What was their style and attitude toward money? What would you change and what would you like to do the same in your own financial future?

2. How important is saving money and what do you consider a reasonable amount to save each month? Should money be invested or traditionally saved? Do you feel that joint or separate accounts would work best?

3. Should contributions to various accounts (household expenses, savings, investments, etc.) be equal, proportional to each person's income, or determined by some other means that feels fair to both of you?

4. Should all purchases be discussed prior to buying? Is this true for large purchases only, or is there a specific dollar amount that should require a discussion beforehand? If so, what is that amount?

5. Who should be responsible for paying the bills? Should all bills be paid prior to or on their due date? Who opens the mail? Where are bills kept in the home? It's best to schedule specific times to sit down and discuss the financial plan. When and how often does this make sense for you?

6. How should bills or debt from before the marriage be handled? This includes car payments, credit card debt, and student loans. How will you handle it if one of you has substantially more debt than the other?

7. Are one or both of you paying child support? Think about tax returns and 401K plans- Should these remain individual or become joint?

8. How do you feel about lending money to others like friends or family in need? In what circumstances and with what kind of terms/conditions would this be acceptable?

9. If one partner loses their source of income or decides to stay home to raise children, how will your financial picture change, and how will you adjust for that change?

10. How will you invest? Does either partner have specific investment expertise? Should you use a financial advisor or planner? Should one be responsible for investing, or will you make decisions together?

11. Is it okay to accept expensive gifts or money from parents? What if there are strings attached? What strings are acceptable, or not? How do you feel about participating in an investment or business venture with family members? Where do you draw the line – is the use of a beach house okay? What if Daddy wants to give his "little girl" a new car? What if one set of parents is much more generous (or affluent) than the other? Could this cause hard feelings?

12. How do you feel about charitable contributions, and how much of your money should be donated to charity? What causes do you want to support?

By working through this list, first individually and then together, you'll both have a very clear picture of your partner's financial history, current situations, values, goals and plans. This will help you as a couple to move forward feeling informed, less vulnerable and confident that you can resolve your differences as they arise. If for some reason these questions bring you to the conclusion that you will never feel the same or get along when it comes to money, that is something worth finding out long before you say, "I do!"

Chapter Three

Children and Pets

"Getting a dog is like getting married. It teaches you to be less self-centered, to accept sudden surprising outbursts of affection, and not to be upset by a few scratches on your car."
Will Stanton

A few years ago, a young couple came to my office with a huge problem. She absolutely wanted children and he absolutely did not. I asked if they had discussed this before getting married, and to my surprise - they said they had! Both seemed to believe that the other would find such bliss in marriage, that it would compel them to give in on the child issue.

What were they thinking? Marriage does not change a person's basic values. There are "kid people" and there are people who have no desire for children. It became clear that there was no room for compromise. Although they remained friends, they went their separate ways. She eventually adopted a child on her own.

Many people think of their pets as children. I myself am an animal person. "Love me, love my dogs," is truly my motto. This is non-negotiable; a deal-breaker. It's okay that others may not feel the same, but I couldn't live with someone who wasn't okay with my pets. Consider this carefully, if it matters to you. No one can fully predict the ways in which a pet will affect your relationship.

Kira & Mark's Story

Kira and Mark first met while Kira was walking Ramona, her toy poodle. They were in a park where Mark played baseball with friends on weekends. It wasn't long before Kira was out there with Ramona, rooting for the team. Although Mark generally liked bigger, heartier dogs like the lab/shepherd mutt he'd grown up playing frisbee with, he thought Ramona was sweet, and he definitely liked Kira!

Mark and Kira got along quite well most of the time, and after a while they moved in together. Almost immediately after merging their two homes into one, Mark was home alone with Ramona and she went stiff. He thought the poodle had had a stroke and, in fact, thought she had died; but after a few seconds she came to and began wandering around, as if in a daze. During this time Ramona had no control over her bodily functions and peed all over the floor. Mark rushed her to the vet right away.

The vet told Mark and Kira that Ramona had suffered an epileptic seizure, and that it was something that could happen just once, or might begin to happen more often. They would have to wait and see.

As time went on, it looked like the seizure was a one-time fluke event, but then two or three months later, it happened again. Then it began to happen more frequently, every 5 or 6 weeks. Mark and Kira's sleep was disrupted every time Ramona moved in the night, because they would react as if she were possibly going into a convulsion.

The veterinarian put Ramona on medication, but it didn't work. After trying two more ineffective treatments, another vet prescribed potassium bromide. That worked, but it had to be specially compounded at a pharmacy. Needless to say, the bills started to mount.

At first Mark felt as Kira did, that it was worth every penny to get the epilepsy under control and give Ramona a normal life. She was indeed a member of the family. However, over time, her seizures became more frequent, requiring more frequent medications. This became a problem for Kira and Mark in terms of juggling their schedules and before long, they were leaving Ramona at a doggy daycare facility to make sure she got the help she needed. Mark was getting worried at the amount of money it was costing to keep Ramona alive, and also concerned about her diminishing quality of life.

Kira was determined to leave no stone unturned when it came to Ramona's care. She was prepared to go into debt, if need be. This difference in attitude about the amount of time and money spent on their pet caused frequent arguments between Mark and Kira. When the vet informed them that Ramona had developed heart disease and would require additional medication to help reduce the fluids in her body, Mark gently suggested that maybe the time had come to think about putting Ramona to sleep.

Kira flipped out, seeing Mark as some kind of monster that would let an innocent animal die without trying everything possible to save her. From Mark's point of view, his life with Kira now revolved almost exclusively around Ramona's health issues. He didn't want to be the bad guy, but he felt that Kira was blaming him for a terrible situation, and it was destroying their relationship.

The most difficult moment for a pet owner to face is when a beloved animal is fatally sick. For some, there is no question about trying everything medically available to prolong the pet's life, but not everyone reacts the same way to this circumstance. Some people are raised with a firm distinction between pets and members of the family. They wouldn't spend the same amount of time or money on pets as on a child.

Differences in caring for pets are not limited to handling illness or extreme situations. Fighting and resentment can occur over decisions as minor as the treats you buy or groomer you choose. Some pet owners feel strongly that their pet should have the best of everything (plush bedding, gourmet treats, organic food, etc.), while other people set limits on treats, toys, and visits to the groomer. These seemingly small matters are all potential issues for conflict in your relationship, but you can avoid a lot of arguing and bickering when you start and proceed on the same page.

Chapter Three: Children and Pets

Whenever a conflict arises over basic values, the best first step is to listen to each other's position and not insist that that your partner's position must change. From this open and respectful starting point, you can begin to reach a compromise. With this approach, rather than adversaries facing each other in a show-down, you become two members of the same team solving a problem together.

For Kira and Mark, Ramona didn't last much longer. She was a very sick dog and all the medication took a toll on her tiny body. The rift between Kira and Mark is still healing. They know that one day they will likely want another pet, because they both miss what Ramona brought to their lives and their home; but they've agreed to frankly discuss all the issues that might cause conflict ahead of time, before they choose their next pet.

Whether or not you have pets, just when you think you've worked out your marital rhythm and balance, more often than not, children come along. Children change just about every-thing, in a marriage and in the household. If you prepare your-selves emotionally for the many inevitable changes that come with raising offspring, your ability to adapt will be stronger.

Children have demands of their own. They require significant amounts of time; time that you're used to spending either alone, together as a couple, or with friends and family. Children can't be left at home alone while you go to work or out to dinner. As a parent, you are committed to selflessness and sacrifice; essen-tially borrowing time, attention and energy from other areas of your life. As your emotions, focus, stamina and other resources are redirected toward children, there is no way around the fact that this major life-change is disrupting.

Whatever egalitarian balance you and your partner settle into before children, it's likely that once children arrive, your roles will tend toward the traditional.

Two-career couples are now the norm. As society changes and women's roles evolve, there will be a redefinition of how common household and childrearing duties are handled. In most modern cultures, fathers today want to be involved with family life. They are present to nurture a strong, intimate bond with their children. This can mean making choices that put family before career opportunities - for instance, turning down overtime or an extra assignment. For men who have grown up with an image of Dad going to work each day as sole provider for the family, this can be a real conflict. It takes effort to balance and honor traditional values with contemporary desires.

Women struggle with their own balancing challenges. Although many moms continue to work outside the home after children are born, they also carry a traditional image of their role in the family. This image of what a mom is "supposed to be" is often more than a modern day's work schedule will permit. It simply isn't possible for a person working full-time to also do all the household chores and all the work related to raising healthy, bright, happy children. When financial responsibilities for supporting the home are shared, the responsibilities for household and family must be shared as well.

When couples prioritize work/life balances together, it's much easier to craft an agreeable system. Keep in mind that as children grow and develop their own social lives, schedules must remain flexible to accommodate changing demands on family time.

Naturally, building a family together is about much more than simply having children or pets. Yes, it's about parenting, but also household chores, creating a safe and comfortable environment, living a healthy lifestyle, setting a good example, taking time for fun, making time to learn, managing money, and countless other considerations that go with family development. From the moment a child (or puppy, or kitten) is brought into the home, family dynamics change. Who will get up in the middle of the night for a 3 AM feeding? Who will walk the dog at 5am in winter, or change the litter box, or clean spills and messes?

Where do you each stand on discipline? I've worked with many couples where one parent is strict while the other is lenient. This is a recipe for disaster, because children, even at a very young age, learn to play you against each other. As strange as it may feel to discuss how you plan to raise children even before you get married – it is essential to do so.

Discuss how you'll handle school issues – how much should a parent intervene, and how much should a child be left to handle situations on his/her own? Do you want your children to go to public, parochial, or private schools? Do you believe that children should be "seen and not heard?" Or do you welcome thoughts, ideas and stories from children and young adults at the dinner table, or holiday parties?

How do you feel about allowances? What is the right age to begin, or end allowance? Should children be obligated to complete certain chores, or given the freedom to decide how much they want to help? What chores are reasonable at five, nine or thirteen years of age? Will your kids be allowed to spend all of their allowance at once, or do you see weekly stipends as a way to teach them about immediate gratification vs. saving for long-term, larger desires?

When they are old enough, do you expect your children to have summer or part time jobs, or are you of the mind that says, "They're only kids once. Let them enjoy their youth." Should young adults contribute to their college education? Will you stand back to let them make their own choices for college?

Someone once told me that he'd pay the entire tab for any of his children to go to college – as long as they chose his Alma Mater. Otherwise, they were on their own. What do you think of this?

Who will make the rules for your children? Who will enforce them? Most importantly, do you agree that it's best to discuss rules for your home in advance and enforce them as a united front? Will your children (young or teens) have a say in this? What about family meetings? As your kids get older, how much responsibility should they be given? Be sure to discuss things like dating, driving, curfews, etc.

How do you plan to handle discipline? What degree of importance will you place on good grades or participation in sports? What if you have a child with special needs? Every child is different; and each son or daughter will handle rules, responsibilities, money, etc. differently. You will surely need to make adjustments to fit each child and current local norms. What's important is that you as parents agree on basic underlying principles, so your children will have clear and consistent boundaries.

Daycare, babysitting, and summer camp are other considerations worth addressing. Do you share the same values about whether or not both parents should work outside the home? How will you select babysitting options? Should children at a certain age go to sleep away camp, or maybe spend a month at Grandma's house during the summer?

Tony & Katie's Story

Tony and Katie had been married for four years when I met them. They had two dogs whom they lovingly referred to as their "kids." When they decided to graduate from puppy parenting to the real thing, a host of new issues caused some rude awakening.

Katie had grown up in a modest home. Her parents, although attentive and loving, had not been overly protective or indulgent with Katie and her brothers. They allowed them to grow up and move away, each in their own due time. At a certain point, Katie's parents had become friends more than authority figures.

As a result of this early environment, Katie developed a strong sense of freedom, independence and responsibility for herself. She bought her own car (with some help) at the age of 16. She also took out loans for college, earned allowance for chores, and moved out of her childhood home by the time she was twenty. Katie had grown up taking little for granted; always given what she needed, but earning what she wanted.

Tony's childhood home had been significantly different. Tony and his brother were catered to by their mother. She cooked three complete, homemade meals every day, drove them everywhere, ironed their school clothes each night and even made up their beds each day, without requesting any help. Both boys were given brand new cars at the age of 16. They never had to pay any college expenses, and were given an allowance each week to use for dates and/or gasoline. Tony's parents even paid for his car insurance, along with his brother's. Neither of the boys had any responsibilities or bills to pay. They both lived at home until they were 27 years old and went straight from their childhood home to married life.

Tony and Katie's big problems started when their children were born. Katie believed that children needed discipline and boundaries, as well as a routine. Tony's approach was to give the kids freedom; he indulged their every whim. Tony began saving every dime to pay for cars and college, often meaning sacrifice for himself and Katie. The children were first and foremost, in everything; and on top of his own doting, Tony's parents routinely indulged their grandchildren with candy, treats and elaborate gifts.

When Katie declared that chores were necessary, Tony accused her of being overly serious and no fun. In reality,

Tony was ill-equipped to handle any household duties himself, so finances and chores were left for Katie to handle. Katie was also home with the children 90% of the time, trying to establish and respect a consistent routine. When Daddy came home, regardless of whether it was bedtime or there was homework left to do, Tony would excite the kids and encourage play time, which distracted the children and disrespected the household routine Katie was working on. The kids easily picked up on the disagreement and quickly sided with Tony. Over time, this caused resentment and an ever-increasing divide in the marriage.

When Tony and Katie first started dating, she often felt jealous that Tony's parents were so generous. She wished that someone had given her a new car – and yet, when Tony's parents would hover over them in a smothering way, Katie realized how much she preferred her own parents' style. She liked being independent, so she never felt obligation.

Although several warning signs had presented themselves at every turn in the road, Katie had ignored them – never guessing that when their own children arrived, Tony would naturally parent them in the only manner he had ever known. The growing conflict between them created major issues in the marriage. Katie perceived an awful lack of respect from both the children and Tony. She felt like she was up against a mountain, until she could take no more.

When I confronted Tony and Katie about the differences in their parenting styles, they admitted that they had never even talked about it. They had both taken their insight from how they'd parented their "dog kids" through the years, and equally assumed that *real* children would be just as easy.

Katie & Tony, like many couples with children, felt strongly that it was important to stay together and work things out, "for the sake of the family." They began an open dialogue and tried to better understand each others' positions. Compromises were made. Katie tried to be less rigid, and Tony backed his wife, to help with the discipline. Household chores were divided fairly; and Tony and the children all found new appreciation for Katie once they saw first-hand how much she'd been accomplishing on her own. The dialogue continues, and often they are back in the office with another parenting issue, but progress has been made.

At what age is it okay for your daughter to start wearing makeup? When are teens old enough to date, and what happens if you don't like the boy or girl your child is dating? Where do you stand on curfews? How do you feel about teenage drinking? Is it okay with you if your teenager has a glass of wine with the family at Thanksgiving? How about drinking at the home of a friend? Does it matter to you that it's illegal? Where do you draw the line?

Today, parenting also includes considerations that impact privacy and safety. When do you allow your child to have a Facebook page? Will you allow unsupervised internet access? At what age? When can they have their own cell phones? How much personal information are they allowed to post on social media sites? How carefully will you monitor all of this?

"In every marriage more than a week old,
there are grounds for divorce.
The trick is to find and continue to find grounds for marriage."
Robert Anderson

June & Keith's Story

June & Keith had a great marriage. They had three children and things were working out well in their family. When the children got to be school age, they wanted a family dog. Keith said, "Sure, why not?" – but June was strongly against it. With no explanation, her answer was a flat out, "NO!"

Keith completely ignored June's adamant wishes and took the kids to the local humane society. They came home with a playful black lab mix, and named him "Max." Max was delightful; great with the children, house trained and friendly. He was the perfect family pet.

June reacted to Max's arrival with hysterics and tears. She was incensed that Keith had paid no attention at all to her requests. Keith was confused by June's behavior, but June could hardly explain it. Unfortunately, the dog issue threatened to tear them apart.

It shocked and gravely disappointed me to hear that Keith had not only defied June's wishes, but also included the children in defying them. Amazingly, this didn't seem to be June's biggest concern. As they sat in my office, June began sobbing. Her tears were heartfelt and neither I nor Keith understood. Then, in one single outburst, she said "Misty."

Apparently, June had also grown up with a black lab. The dog's name was "Misty." Misty died on Christmas Eve when June was thirteen years old. Misty had been June's best friend, her loyal companion and to the present day, the dog held a very special spot in June's heart. When Misty died, a part of June had died with her. June's parents didn't ever validate her grief. They basically told her to "get over it" and get another dog.

At last, after this important piece of June's history poured forth, Keith understood. June didn't want their children to experience loss like she had. She didn't want to ever stop grieving Misty. June had never quite gotten over her childhood dog's death, and bringing a new dog, especially a similar breed, into their current home only brought all of June's sadness back.

I helped Keith understand that it is never okay to make a unilateral decision without June's consent - especially a decision like getting a puppy, which brings significant long-term implications that affect everyone in the family. After we worked on solutions for them as a couple, June continued to see me alone. She wanted to understand her own feelings and finally heal from the death of her childhood pet, Misty.

In time, June developed a wonderful and healthy relationship with Max. As it turned out, she was elated about having a new canine companion in their home. What's interesting here is that although June & Keith had started dating when they were only eighteen, Keith had never heard anything about Misty. The subject of former pets had never come up before Max entered their lives.

Second marriages can pose particular challenges to negotiating childrearing; as there is often insecurity around the new 'step' parent's role. Quite frequently, it isn't only children who need to be negotiated, but also an extended family of ex-spouses, ex-in-laws and old family friends who affect second marriages as life goes on.

Judy and Pat's Story

When they met and fell in love, Judy and Pat each had two children from previous marriages. Both were busy professionals who had worked out cordial relationships with their exes for shared custody and visitation. Each had their kids about half the time, and their exes were both reasonably accommodating when flexibility and adjustments to the schedule were needed.

Judy and Pat married and created a blended family with hopes for a peaceful future. The new couple trusted that since there had been no major problems with their children's other parents before, it would be fairly easy to blend the two families after marriage. This turned out to be completely wrong.

Pat's son had a severe developmental disorder that caused him to sometimes be socially inappropriate. He would talk constantly, interrupting other people with inane questions and chatter. This drove Judy crazy!

Judy's two children were very precocious – some might say TOO precocious. They were already engaging in dating and drinking behavior more appropriate for people five years older. Judy was fine with early experimenting because she too, had been an early bloomer. Pat, however, didn't like his young teens being exposed to such adult behaviors (and lack of restrictions). The fact that all four were relatively close in age didn't help.

Another challenge they hadn't predicted was lack of privacy – with each other, and each with their own children. Their goal was to have everyone together for a few days each week, as well as a few days each week for the two of them alone. However, when they had all four kids at once, it was chaos. Pat and Judy had a few days each week alone, but neither of them had much separate time with their own children.

When they tried having Pat's kids for part of each week and Judy's for the other part, they didn't feel like much of a family, and the children had hardly any interaction with each other. It seemed that no matter how many ways they tried to compromise, there was no successful remedy for this dilemma. Judy once confessed that, had she known how difficult blending their families would be, she wouldn't have married Pat.

Blending families is almost never easy, even under the best of circumstances. Is it okay to discipline (or set rules for) a child that is not yours by birth? Is it okay to enforce different standards for different children who live within the same household? What if the children don't get along? What if they resent the intrusion of a step-parent, when they used to have Mom or Dad all to themselves?

Chapter Three: Children and Pets

In Pat and Judy's case, there were four cooperative adults who all wanted what was best for the children. Unfortunately, that is often not the circumstance in blended families. Many times one parent will try to use the children against the other, or say disparaging things about a new spouse who becomes the step-parent. Over the years, I have seen some very ugly step-parenting situations, when adults were not able to put their issues aside, even for the benefit of their children.

Discussion is always important before getting married, but never more so than when blending families. Juggling your own schedule plus the schedules of children and ex-spouses is truly daunting. Come to an understanding up front of how schedules will work. Determine your agreed rules about privacy, discipline, chores and family time, remembering that it's crucial for all to remain flexible, because you must be able to accommodate changing schedules as well as special circumstances.

If you are living now with your partner's children, give them and yourself some time to get to know each other. The fewer expectations you have, the more likely you'll be to create a comfortable relationship based on mutual respect. It's important to be consistent with children, so even if they are distant at times, be sure to remain steady instead of reacting or withdrawing yourself.

Showing love to their parent you live with and respect to the other parent is a great way to set their minds at ease and open them up to trusting you. You will, over time, forge your own relationship with stepchildren. In the meantime, try to remember how difficult it is for them to be without their other biological parent. Show some compassion. Assure stepchildren that you understand how important that relationship is. Let them know that there's no reason to ever feel that their original parental bonds are threatened.

Generally, it's best to discuss concerns about discipline with your partner, so that the birth parent is the one to consistently implement changes or penalties. If there are children from both partners, or a new baby as well as children from a previous marriage, strive as much as possible to be fair to all the children in your household.

You cannot account for or control the behavior of an ex-spouse; you can only decide to support your stepchildren in any way that you can. It will help your stepchildren and the flow of your new family life to have a sense of solidarity in your new marriage. The more you and your spouse discuss important issues and agree on the best ways to proceed, the more likely you will all be to paddle in the same direction, and harmony will prevail.

Setting boundaries around your marriage will offer a degree of solace and security, no matter what the extenuating circumstances. Remember to set aside alone time for you and your partner. Keep in mind all the things you did as a couple that felt special and kept you close in the beginning. Remember also to set aside time for just your family to be together, without other family members. Create traditions of your own together.

Questions to Consider and Discuss About Children & Pets

1. Do you want children? If so, how many? Do you care about the gender of the child? Are you flexible in your wishes? Why or Why not?

2. If you discover that one of you can't have children naturally, would you explore medical intervention? Consider a surrogate mother or sperm donor? How do you feel about adoption?

3. If your child is born with special needs, how much are you prepared to sacrifice? Are you willing to compromise time, finances and attention normally devoted to other family members? How far will you go to meet the needs of a child with extraordinary physical or mental disabilities?

4. Are animals important to you? Do you feel that having pets around the home enhances the family unit? Should pets be kept indoors or outdoors? Explain your childhood history with pets.

5. What were the roles of your mother and father when you were growing up in their home? What did you wish you could change? In what ways would you like to be a similar parent and what do you want to do differently with your own children?

6. Discuss discipline. Do you believe in spanking? Were you spanked? What forms of "teaching a lesson" or punishment are acceptable to you? How much involvement should grandparents have in teaching and disciplining your children?

7. Development and Education: How do you feel about sending your child to daycare? Do you want your child to attend pre-school, or wait to begin in kindergarten?

8. Do you want your child to play sports? Are you ok with football and/or hockey, or do you prefer track, swimming or soccer because they're "safer?" Do you want to give your child piano and art lessons? Do you hope he/she will pursue a career in the theater, or join the military?

9. Do you agree that it is essential to form and respect a united front? When you disagree with one another regarding a boundary, rule, or discipline of your children, how will it be handled? What are the most important things when it comes to parenting that you both want to implement, or avoid?

10. If you are considering a blended family, how will you balance the autonomy of each family unit, while still being fair to all? How will you handle the situation if one ex-spouse is uncooperative, or worse?

11. How will you as parents stay united and be there for your children when life throws inevitable curve balls?

"Parenthood is a lot easier to get into than out of!"
Bruce Lansky

Chapter Four

Religion, Politics and Core Values

Relationships have long been fueled on friendly rivalries that can involve something playful, like collegiate football favorites. A house divided in this situation is not that serious and can actually add a lighthearted sense of competition and disagreement to the mix. However, when rivalry is based on or around core values, the result can be much less than friendly. Resentment, anger and frustration can build.

Surprisingly, many couples never discuss pertinent topics like religion and politics prior to marriage. Then, suddenly there are children and one partner is determined to go to church and enroll the kids in Sunday school, while the other partner is wondering where all this interest in religion came from.

There is an endless list of values (beyond religion and politics) that might be different or potentially cause conflict. For example, how do you each feel about public vs. private vs. parochial vs. home schooling for your children? How would you handle an unwanted/unplanned pregnancy? What if one of your kids announced that he or she was gay?

The trick is to figure out where you both stand on meaningful life issues <u>before</u> entering into a long term relationship. Let's first make it clear that it is not necessary to be in total agreement with each other on all matters. Political pundits James Carville and Mary Matalin are an example of a married couple who have diametrically opposed political views, but they've been together as a family (a very public family) for many years. Carville and Matalin have obviously figured out a way to get past their differences; and so can you, once you figure out exactly what your differences are.

Tolerance for differences is really what's at issue here. Some people are naturally tolerant and truly embrace the idea that "variety is the spice of life." They find that not always thinking and feeling the same, keeps things "interesting." Others learn to take a somewhat "*c'est la vie*" attitude about differences, as a result of what they've learned through life experiences. Flexibility and acceptance can go a long way toward peace and happiness, but for some individuals, "right" is right and "wrong" is wrong, and there is no point discussing any other opinion. If you and your partner are not able to respect each other's differences, this is a huge red flag for your relationship.

> *"Marriage is an alliance entered into by*
> *a man who can't sleep with the window shut and*
> *a woman who can't sleep with the window open..."*
> George Bernard Shaw

Keep in mind that there are many happy inter-racial families, mixed-religion families and families where one partner is a "health nut" while the other is a "junk-food junkie." There are even households where one spouse is a Democrat and the other, a Republican. These and many other couples make their relationships work in spite of their differences, but there are also countless couples who fall apart over the same issues.

Phil and Rick's Story

Phil and Rick had constant disputes about Rick's insistence on buying organic foods. Phil thought they were unnecessarily expensive, but what presented initially as a money conflict was really a conflict about values.

In Phil's family growing up there were five children, so there'd always been an emphasis on stretching food dollars. Phil's mom used coupons and made dinners from whatever was on sale. From Phil's point of view, if Rick could spend less on food, there'd be more money for other things.

Rick had not had the same experience in childhood. Although he and his sister often went shopping with their mom and watched her compare items according to price, Rick's mom also emphasized good nutrition. Her philosophy was that it was better to spend a little more for healthy foods than to "save" on junk filled with empty calories. From Rick's point of view, it wasn't a good idea to skimp on food quality. Rick cared deeply about the health of his family. He also believed buying food locally was a way of supporting his community.

Once Rick explained to Phil all the reasons why he made the grocery decisions he made, they were able to reach a compromise of spending on organic foods while also cutting other spending for an easier-to-handle grocery budget. They were able to negotiate their middle ground successfully once Phil saw the reasons behind Rick's thinking.

Core value differences and an inability to compromise or accept these differences will cast long shadows on a marriage. Take a look at the following questions. Ask them of yourself and your partner. Even if one conflict seems unlikely right now, keep it in the mix, to see what kind of response you both have. If grave disagreement arises, imagine spending your life with some-one who feels so differently from you. Using your left-brain to analyze cognitively vs. your right-brain's emotions, try to decide whether or not you can live with fundamental opposition in the long term.

How important is formal education to you? What about less formal – such as personal growth education? Do you support your partner in his/her quest for self improvement through education? Does your partner support you in the same ways?

How aligned are your respective work ethics? Is your partner a nine to fiver putting in minimum hours to collect a paycheck? Are you a Type A workaholic –passionate about what you do and devoting endless hours to it? Do you respect and encourage each other's work habits, or secretly resent them? It's import-ant to explore these feelings and bring them out into the open before they cause rifts between you.

How important is a healthy lifestyle to you and your part-ner? Do you live on fast food while your mate will only touch organic salads? Consider smoking, drinking alcohol, pot smoking (or other drugs). What do you each consider "recreation" vs. abuse? Are you comfortable with one another's habits and activities? How do you complement each other when it comes to exercise, yoga or meditation? Are your compatible in these lifestyle routines?

Let us not forget or ignore the dynamic duo of religion and politics. While these may not be subjects to bring up in conversation with casual acquaintances, they are certainly important discussions to have with your partner before committing to marriage.

To a large extent, many of these are personality issues and a certain amount of our personality may be hard wired (just ask the mother of twins who have distinctly different temperaments, in spite of coming from the same gene pool and an identical early childhood environment). The most important point here is to know which kind of personality *you* are, so you can determine what other personality types you can live with.

If you tend to be judgmental, you'll need to be with someone who sees the world very much the way you do; someone whose behaviors and interests generally mirror your own. In other words, you must first be honest with yourself about how much difference you can tolerate, and then make sure your intended is coming from a similar place.

Remember that while some differences can be exciting in the early stages of a relationship, they may take you too far out of your comfort zone in the long term. Don't forget that in the beginning, you are on a dopamine high, oblivious to the internal workings of the person you are with. As the high wears off you may see, find, feel and be put off by personality issues that clash profoundly with your own. How much difference can each of you tolerate, and how simple or hard is it to reach agreeable compromise?

"Strike an average between what a woman thinks of her husband a month before she marries him and what she thinks of him afterward, and you will have the truth about him."
H.L. Mencken, 1916

Lisa & Ted's Story

Lisa and Ted met through mutual friends. Ted is a real outdoorsman, loving long hikes and backpacking, camping out in tents, etc. Lisa enjoys the luxuries of resorts with well appointed spas, but she found Ted's outdoorsy interests fun and different. Lisa loved walks in the woods – as long as it was a beautiful spring day and the mosquitoes hadn't yet emerged for the season. Even sleeping in the tent was fun; listening to crickets chirping and snuggling in a sleeping bag for two.

Lisa loved Ted and they shared many of the same values, hopes and dreams, so they got married and began a life together. After a year or two, Ted's outdoor adventures lost their appeal for Lisa. She was still happy to take the occasional walk in the woods on a beautiful day, but she resented the time spent camping out when she could have been doing something more enjoyable with her precious down time. Tent camping lost its appeal when Lisa had to go without her Starbuck's the next morning!

Chapter Four: Religion, Politics and Core Values

It wasn't long before Ted was going off with some friends for weekend trips. Lisa spent her leisure time alone, since most of her girlfriends were married and doing couples' things.

When Ted and Lisa came to me for help, they were afraid that their marriage was headed for divorce. They were no longer spending quality time together and each resented the other's lack of interest in activities they valued. We reviewed the many things they still share in common, and the dreams they each have for the future. It turned out that they both enjoy skiing and sailing, and there are deluxe accommodations at many national parks. Their compromise is that Ted goes on short camping trips with friends twice a year, and they also vacation together as a couple in locations where they can both find something to enjoy. In this way, they hope to increase the area of common ground between them.

In spite of their mutual efforts to compromise, the difference between them looms large. We all work hard, all year long. Most Americans have only a few weeks each year to enjoy precious, hard-earned leisure time. Lisa is not happy about the prospect of spending vacation weeks alone, and she's not sure she'll like vacationing in a national park at all, no matter how many luxurious options there are. Ted is worried that he won't have the opportunity to relax the way he likes to. The negotiations for Ted and Lisa continue, so that each can have space to do the things they love, without causing their partner to feel neglected.

If the reason for separate vacations is not to avoid being together, then time apart need not be threatening. As long as there is also time for shared vacations, there are occasions when it might be perfectly appropriate to vacation separately. There is no reason to give up a destination you've always dreamt about, simply because your partner doesn't share enthusiasm for that location. If and when you do travel alone, discuss safety concerns before departure, so your mate won't need to worry. Make it easy to stay in touch with each other when apart.

If you're meeting with old friends or family, perhaps for a reunion, it's okay to go alone when your partner has no interest in or connection to those people. That said, don't just assume your partner isn't interested in joining you. Give him/her the option to attend, so neither of you ever feel left out, but if they choose to stay behind, don't let that keep you from going, doing, seeing or experiencing what matters to you. Sharing your life with someone else doesn't have to mean giving up your own life. You can enjoy many things with your lover and still have some things that you love to do by, or for, yourself.

Perhaps you don't have a specific activity to attend, but simply need an afternoon to yourself. Don't feel guilty! It's okay to take some time alone. The most important thing is to fully discuss your needs and desires, while listening (and really hearing) your partner's desires as well. Caring doesn't have to mean bending or changing, but it does mean wanting your spouse to be happy. When you give one another the space to achieve individual fulfillment, you are more likely to be content and successful as a couple.

If your partner is dead set against separate vacations, explore the reasons why. Is it because of a lack of trust? Does your partner hate to be alone? Try to get to the heart of the matter and address core concerns. Each partner needs space within the relationship to follow his or her own pursuits. When you each feel that your own needs are being met, you can engage with confidence and fully nurture each other.

Speaking of space – this can be a huge issue for couples. Many people think that getting married means spending all non-working time with their partner. Others are very clear that they don't want to be attached at the hip. In general, men are socialized to 'go it alone,' and autonomy is their holy grail. Women, on the other hand, are generally socialized to care more about their connections to family and friends, and particularly desire an intimate connection with a mate.

When you're living with a partner after years of living alone, you'll often find that your privacy needs change. Before you lived together, you wanted to spend all your free time together, but now that you share the same living space, you need to stake out time and room for privacy. If one of you needs a lot of togetherness while the other needs a lot of space, it's wise to pay attention to those values. Compromise may work for a while, but a difference in comfort level regarding personal space is a huge red flag, and often, one or both people will eventually feel over-compromised.

Transitioning from being mostly alone to mostly together may seem easy, but it can also feel threatening. One thing to realize is that love and the growing intimacy between you will bring up all your craziness, fears and neuroses. As Gay Hendricks puts it in *Conscious Loving*, "love shines a powerful light on your relationship, and it will likely cast an intense shadow, too."

It's scary to reveal your inner truths to another person. It can make anyone feel vulnerable; like love means giving up control. You may fear that if you are known for the person you truly are, warts and all, your partner will want to run away. Sometimes people run from each other to avoid deeper sharing of their inner selves, because it's easier to bury these fears than to face them.

On the other hand, some people fear independence, and are uncomfortable spending time alone. According to Hendricks, "wanting to be together and wanting to be alone sometimes are both important components of a vital intimate relationship, and occur in a natural rhythm." It's important to understand and be in touch with your own needs for connection vs. independence. This will enable you to better cope with and balance your partner's needs.

Workaholism is encouraged in our society as a sign of ambition; or perhaps constant overtime is required to stay ahead of regular bills. Unfortunately, when one person is a workaholic who can find no time for attending to the relationship at home, the relationship will suffer. Establishing a work/life balance that you are both comfortable with is critical to the continued growth of your life together.

People who argue about religion, politics and other core values are forced to revisit their deepest held, most basic beliefs. These frequently derive from one's sense of good versus evil. As stated earlier in this chapter, many people's beliefs about religion and politics are deeply enmeshed with their upbringing. As you explore each other's beliefs, it's important to be diplomatic.

Take great care when you question or challenge the most basic of loyalties - not necessarily to a political party or particular religion, but to family. For most people, this is an even deeper loyalty. There are various allegiances at play in every marriage, both conscious and unconscious, and sometimes they conflict.

"Marriage is that relation between man and woman
in which the independence is equal, the dependence mutual,
and the obligation reciprocal."
Louis Anspacher

Chad & Sue's Story

Chad and Sue had been married for two years when they found their way to my office. Sue was in the midst of a transformation; an unfolding of spirit that was helping her work toward her dream of becoming a holistic health practitioner. Sue had always been interested in the metaphysical, and finally started taking steps to bring her goals to fruition. She was taking classes after work and investing a significant amount of her earnings into her training. She attended weekend workshops, took home study courses and apprenticed with several people who were supporting her journey to do healing energy work.

Chad quite simply thought that Sue had lost her mind. He accused her of doing voodoo and denying her Christian upbringing. A committed Christian himself, Chad saw Sue's pursuits as wicked. He simply could not, or would not, accept it. The more time Sue spent on developing her skills, the more upset and closed off Chad became. Sue tried endlessly to explain, but each time, they would argue. Chad would dismiss her, saying that the "witchcraft" had gone to her head.

Before the marriage, Sue had often read metaphysical and holistic healing books; they cluttered her home. Chad would pick them up and toss them aside, calling them crazy. Sue had decided that she wouldn't discuss this side of herself with Chad anymore, to avoid his hurtful and closed-minded comments. She didn't realize that this very important part of her would rise to the surface after marriage.

Sue did a disservice to both of them by not exploring this issue with Chad. It was obviously important to her, and the red flags were already in place long before they married. Now the two of them were drifting apart because of different core beliefs and values. If Sue had been honest from the beginning about how much the spiritual change and career transition meant to her, instead of pushing an essential conversation out of the way, she might have spared them both a good deal of aggravation and heartache.

The biggest issue with Chad and Sue was that they had no middle ground. In order for Chad to be comfortable in the relationship, Sue would have to give up her dream. Both were committed to their individual beliefs, and as a result of inability to compromise, the marriage suffered. They finally decided it would be best to end their marriage, before bringing children into what was becoming a rather hostile environment.

Although people can change, few of us are able to stray far from the core values embedded in us by our family, social and religious upbringings. If these issues remain under the radar during the dating phase, they will certainly show up once "I do's" are uttered.

Asking questions to understand what makes individuals who they are at deeper levels, is crucial to identifying what will and won't come up over a long-term relationship. Remaining cognizant of differences along the way can open up conversations that will either bridge a compromise, or make people aware that there are rocky paths ahead.

Interfaith couples often minimize the differences they were raised with, because they are so in love. This can lead to trouble later on, especially around holiday time. It's a good idea to probe differences and spend time getting to know all you can about your partner's religion. Try to understand how important faith has been in his/her life, and to what degree it influenced your partner's childhood. Spouses who come from different faiths must discuss and understand each other's religious backgrounds. This is the only way to navigate the future with some degree of assurance, diplomacy and respect.

Be sure to discuss which faith-based traditions you'd each like to observe, either in your early life together, or when you have children. There are holidays such as Chanukah or Christmas, and there are other important faith-based events, like a bris, for instance, or confirmation. One of you may feel strongly about these occasions, or your parents may feel strongly about traditions that they'd like you to continue. It's a good idea to discuss how your faith diverges from your parents', and be clear about what you will or won't do to accommodate your family's commitment to religion.

So, how do Mary Matalin and James Carville do it? With views so diametrically opposed, and on top of that, their very public livelihoods, it seems unlikely that they could maintain a harmonious relationship. Yet, they've been married for more than 20 years. Carville says that in private they avoid discussing politics, since they disagree so completely. Matalin says their success stems from "faith, family and good wine."

The following questions are designed to create and foster open, honest dialogue. Many of the situations are hypothetical, and we certainly can't be prepared for everything, but understanding your partner, not to mention yourself, is a great start. Finding a mutually acceptable middle ground, or knowing (and accepting) yourself well enough to know where and when middle ground is not good enough, can save a lot of heart ache and pain.

Questions about Core Values, Religion and Politics

1. Are you open to spending time apart? Do you need to spend every moment together, or is it comfortable for each to pursue your own activities without risking loss of intimacy?

2. Consider your partner's work routine, ambition and stamina. Will you be okay if your partner works 80 hours a week, or will you begin to feel resentment or jealousy?

3. How do you feel about your partner having friendships with members of the opposite sex that don't always include you?

4. How important is religion to you? Do you go to services regularly? If you have children, will your religious commitments change? How strongly do you feel about your religious beliefs? How important is it that you and your spouse have similar beliefs? Must your children share those beliefs?

5. Is education important to you? How do you feel about your partner continuing his/her education when it will drain time and resources from the marriage? Will you take turns helping and supporting each other through continued education? How do you feel about your children going to college? How will this be paid for?

6. List three things you are not willing to give up for marriage. Explain how you feel about these things and why they are important.

7. Think about the morals instilled in you through your upbringing and discuss them. Could you be married to someone with drastically different political opinions? Can you tolerate drinking and/or smoking? How do you honestly feel about diversity issues – race, gender, etc.? If your child fell in love with someone of the same gender or a different race, culture, religion, etc. – how would you feel about it and handle it?

8. Think about body image and health....Is it important that you always work out and eat right? Do you take care of yourself at all costs? Are you interested in "going green?" Do you recycle? Is it okay with you if your partner follows his/her own choices in these things?

If disagreements arise from answering these questions (and that is quite possible), discuss them in detail. Now is the time to gain knowledge that can affect the remainder of your life together. No one can deal with something that they don't know about.

> *"A long marriage is two people trying to dance a duet and two solos at the same time."*
>
> Anne Taylor Fleming

Chapter Five

Friends, Family and Social Life

Sarah and Paul's Story

Two good friends of mine have had an on again, off again relationship for some time. They truly consider themselves soul mates and anyone who sees them together knows that they share something very special.

Sarah is extremely close to her family. She cannot imagine ever living more than an hour away from her relatives, and considers her mother her best friend. Sarah confides in her mother a lot; revealing intimate details about her relationship with Paul.

Paul is also close to his family and loves them very much, but he feels no need to live in close proximity to them. Paul considers the details of life with Sarah private; just between the two of them. He would never discuss their relationship with his family, or anyone else.

Paul and Sarah both have successful careers, but he wants the freedom to pick up and move anywhere in the country, or even the world, if the right opportunity presents itself. This poses a conflict with Sarah's desire to stay near her family.

These family issues keep Paul and Sarah from getting married. Maybe there will come a time when Sarah doesn't need to have her family so close to her, or maybe someday Paul will be content to settle down in one place. Either way, until the two of them can embrace and appreciate the situation they're in, they are wise not to make a marital commitment.

Second only to money, parents and in-laws seem to be the source of the most problems in relationships. When children are involved, the problems can be tenfold. Be sure to discuss these potential mine fields early on, and prepare for how you will handle such problems, if they arise.

> *"All marriages are happy. It's the living together afterward that causes all the trouble."*
> *Raymond Hull*

In his book, *The Seven Basic Quarrels of Marriage*, psychotherapist William Betcher describes a hierarchy of three kinds of loyalties at work in any close relationship. The first is loyalty to your roots, which encompasses all the beliefs you absorbed, consciously and unconsciously, from your family, your school and the world at large while growing up. These beliefs range from your sense of patriotism, to your determination to back up a sibling, no matter what the circumstance, because you're related. Many times the way you do things - for instance, what you like to do on a holiday - comes from your experience with your family.

The second loyalty is between the two partners in marriage. It involves all the values and ideas you share, the way you agree to handle daily tasks as well as special emergencies, the way you treat confidences between the two of you. It includes faithfulness within your marriage.

The third kind of loyalty in a marriage is loyalty to the marriage itself, to the responsibilities of maintaining a household, of caring for children and taking care of the sick. It is a loyalty to the family that the partners have founded.

These three different loyalties are not always in sync, and often cause trouble. It's important to discuss between you what things separate your current, shared family from your families of origin, and how you will resolve any loyalty conflicts. Remember, talking about family is a sensitive subject that needs to be handled with diplomacy and respect. Loyalties are grown in the heart, not decided upon in the head.

Jay & Karla's Story

Jay and Karla have a picture-perfect marriage, except that Karla is somewhat of a social butterfly. She tries desperately to drag Jay to cocktail parties, drinks with co-workers and family functions on weekends. Jay mostly wants to stay at home and be with Karla alone; without constant interference from friends and family. He finds it difficult to be around many people at once. Jay is also still bitter that Karla's father refused to give her away to him at their wedding.

Jay feels that the dinners every Sunday with Karla's parents only put salt on the wound, but Karla thinks that showing up happy together is the best revenge. Recently, Jay stood his ground and chose not to meet up with Karla after work. He decided to do yard work at home rather than attend Sunday dinners with her parents. This has left them with little time together and a lot of tension between them.

Karla forgives her family for everything, including their shunning of Jay. She is unwilling to curb her social life, declaring that this is their time to be free – to go, do and see whatever they like. Jay disagrees. He thinks partying and visiting with family in moderation is fine, but that it's time for the two of them to start their own family traditions.

There are several problems here. Karla, being so close to her family, cannot see herself or her husband as anything but extensions of them. Furthermore, her social needs are high. Jay on the other hand, is fairly quiet and reserved. He prefers to focus his energy on the life he and Karla are starting.

Resolution for these two is still a work in progress. They are trying to reach acceptable levels of socialization for each of them, and have openly confronted the issues with Karla's father. Apologies were offered and mending of the wounds is beginning. In the meantime, they have committed to spending most Sundays together at home, and save visits to both families for special occasions and holidays.

For Karla and Jay, the warning signs were there long before they got married. Karla's behavior didn't change after they exchanged their vows. Jay simply assumed marriage would change everything. This is unfortunately a grave, yet common mistake. A good rule of thumb is: assume nothing! Marriage does <u>not</u> automatically change people. You will save yourself a lot of pain and wasted time if you accept and understand this before choosing a spouse.

Sometimes it's easy to fall into subconscious habits and routines, especially around members of your family of origin. When these habits interfere with the routines of your marriage, you need to set boundaries and decide when extended family takes precedence (or doesn't). In some cases you'll need to discuss this with your family, so they can understand and respect boundaries you've set for yourself and your relationship. Perhaps you've always gone to your parents' home for birthdays, but now would like to start a tradition of your own. These are rules you need to make up for yourself; there are no right or wrong ways to proceed.

Think about what role your family plays in your life. How much do you want them involved in your marriage? What information is kept private, just between you and your spouse; and what is okay to discuss with family or close friends?

Do you take vacations alone as a couple, or are family and friends always part of the equation? How are holidays divided up between each of your friends and family? How much privacy and independence do you need as a couple?

What happens if one family is very generous with time, help, and money, etc. while the other family is not? Will there be resentment? Does assistance come with strings attached? What if your parents don't like your partner, or your in-laws disagree with how you plan to raise your children? Is blood always thicker than water?

I had a client whose in-laws retired to Orlando, Florida. The in-laws gave their grandkids expensive tickets to Disneyworld for Christmas, without consulting the parents. My client saw this as a manipulative way of forcing the family to visit them by putting them in a position of accepting the gift or disappointing the kids.

This gift also obliged the family to arrange a week of vacation and buy expensive plane tickets. It could have been fine, had the grandparents not taken it upon themselves to give such a gift without consulting the parents. In therapy, the husband agreed to discuss this with his parents and ask them not to give such gifts in the future without discussing it with them first.

Melanie and Mickel's Story

One recent client was considering leaving her husband. He comes from an Eastern European country where children are expected to care for their parents, forever. Often in her husband's homeland, three or four generations of a family live in the same household together. My client (the wife) however, is American through and through, and a very independent woman.

Melanie always resented how Mickel would drop anything he was doing at their home to do some insignificant task at his parents' house. He gives his mother part of his paycheck each month, even though she is employed and self-sufficient. The final straw snapped just a few weeks later, when Mickel's mother announced that she'd decided to retire (at a still very young age), and expected Mickel to contribute an additional $1000 per month to her living expenses.

When Melanie heard this, she hit the ceiling! They are already struggling to pay their own bills. She's finishing graduate school and raising two young children. Mickel's salary is adequate, but not large. The contributions Michel's mother is now requiring will force Mickel and Melanie's children to go without! To Melanie, this is unacceptable.

It seems clear that Mickel will have to make a choice between his wife and his mother, but nothing could cause him greater discomfort. Despite the fact that he dearly loves his wife, and can see her point of view, he cannot bring himself to refuse his mother.

Mikel now has a job offer from another town. Once his mother is no longer a daily source of irritation, it may be easier for Mickel and Melanie to find an acceptable balance between loyalties, but geographical change rarely resolves such issues completely. Mickel's goal is to please his wife without disrespecting his mother or their cultural traditions, and he is still trying to find that balance.

In-laws will most likely be with you for a long time, so it's best to treat them with respect, even if you don't really feel it. Do it for your partner's sake and for greater harmony in your own family life. Even when conflict arises between your partner and his/her own parents, it's better to just listen and try to be supportive, rather than get involved. When the parental conflict is over, your spouse will still feel loyalty to his/her family, and also grateful to you if you haven't said anything nasty about them.

Don't skip sharing stories and memories about your childhood family life. This is part of getting to know each other - understanding who you both are and where you each come from. If you're looking ahead to sharing a life together, you'll be sharing it with your in-laws as well, so it's best to know the situation and understand any unresolved childhood issues from your partner's point of view.

Just as personal boundaries help to maintain an individual's psychological and emotional well-being, so do boundaries between a marriage and the outer world. Obligations to family and friends go a long way to preserve the emotional integrity of a marriage. Discuss your expectations about holidays, vacations, visiting, your family's relationship with your children (if/when you have them), and what you are willing to discuss with your family vs. what should remain private.

Discuss practical issues concerning your in-laws and your own parents, such as health problems and finances. What are their retirement plans? How involved will you need to be in paying for their continued comfort? What kind of care and responsibility are they expecting from you and your family as they age?

If it is particularly difficult to tolerate a partner's family member or dear friend, it is best to discuss this openly, but with a great amount of caution. Don't silently fume when a family member pushes your buttons. Agree on a password to use when you and your partner are in company, so that when you've had all you can take, your partner knows the signal that says it's time to end the visit.

Some of the most basic biological facts need to be taken into consideration here. Women are biologically designed to think differently from men about familial and friendship connections. According to psychologist Carol Gilligan, "women are hard-wired for affiliations; for maintaining connections to others, whether family, friends, or the community. Men see danger in interdependence, and indeed our society as a whole glorifies autonomy, while denigrating dependence on others in any way."

A woman may be accustomed to confiding in her friend, but her disclosures may feel like a betrayal to her husband. The consequence could be that he stops telling her personal things, for fear that she'll discuss them with a third party. If you'd rather keep some personal things private, you need to have that understanding between you. Negotiate and set the rules of your relationship together.

One family issue might be deciding when the two of you will have "alone time." A new wife may not be as happy as a former wife when your kids spend a lot of time with your parents. Many family conflicts are about boundaries. Boundaries must be set and respected. If you like privacy or feel invaded when life constantly revolves around family – then marrying an open book who loves having family around may be rough.

While no relationship is perfect 100% of the time, it's wise to select a partner you have more in common with vs. less. Compatibility not only makes life easier, but takes a load of pressure off, because you can be yourself without concern that you will upset or inconvenience your mate. If you are already in a committed relationship as you read this, don't worry! These chapters and the essential conversations they facilitate will dramatically improve your understanding of yourself; and subsequently, communication between you.

You may have no problem with a boys' night out, but how do you feel about your husband's lunches with a female friend? When you create a game plan to confront big issues before marriage, you will both be better prepared as conflicts arise. At the very least, you will clearly know exactly where your partner stands on sensitive matters. It is only when you know and understand each other that you can weather occasional storms for a successful union.

Conflict can sometimes present itself as you try to strike a work/life balance. You may feel loyalty to your company that keeps you putting in extra hours. Being successful in today's workforce means reaching beyond the status quo. If you travel for your work, perhaps more travel would help you move ahead. When both spouses feel strongly about pursuit of thriving careers, it may prove difficult to find time to devote to your relationship. If one partner is hardly motivated, simply putting in time for a paycheck while the other is a workaholic consumed with his/her career, this can certainly cause conflict down the line, especially if you decide to have children.

Statistics say that individuals who are married to their work will not stay long in a relationship. Marriages where one partner is a workaholic are twice as likely to end in divorce. When you make a commitment to spend your time with your spouse, leave your work behind- no emails, no calls. Focus on your partner and remind yourself why you're grateful for your loving relationship.

If you're married to a workaholic, try to understand why your spouse is addicted to work. The more you understand (and the less you challenge or attack his/her choices), the more your partner will be comfortable to share with you, which will help you both to relax better at home.

Workaholism is not an excuse to shirk family and household responsibilities. If you agree to take out the trash, then take out the trash. If you are the partner of a workaholic, don't delay family activities because you're waiting for your spouse to join you; this only enables more workaholism. If dinner is at 6 and your spouse isn't home, go ahead and eat. If the kids go to sleep at 9 PM, put them to sleep at 9 PM.

This is not about punishing your hard-working spouse; it is merely a way to keep the family running smoothly around him/her when they are not able or willing to support household routines. This also does not have to apply when your partner works occasional overtime or has a special project deadline.

Try to balance supporting your mate's professional goals with meeting your family's needs. Consider and discuss what you each see as the difference between being a responsible, dedicated professional vs. a workaholic taking advantage of family time for personal gain. Sometimes a parent is working extra hours specifically FOR the family; to afford extracurricular activities for children or a special vacation, etc. Be mindful that a responsible, dedicated professional can also be a responsible, devoted parent.

There are times when a wife who stays at home wants to take a lovely (and much deserved) vacation. She also wants to remodel the kitchen and finish the basement. Don't forget that lovely piece of jewelry she has her eye on for Christmas... These things are all fine and dandy, but if this same wife complains that her husband works too many hours, she needs to consider her wish list. Does she want more time with her husband at home, or does she want him to hustle so they can afford luxurious extras in life? We can't have it all, and everyone needs to find a healthy bending point to make marriage fair. You need to decide for the two of you what boundaries work best in your home, and adjust along the way as needed.

Questions about Family, Friends & Social Life

1. Do you like each others' friends? How often do you like to socialize? How much time should you spend, together and separately, with friends? How much leisure time should be for just the two of you?

2. How do you feel about your partner's family? Do they accept you? If not, does it bother you? Do you feel that your partner sees his/her family too often, or too infrequently? What is the perfect balance for you?

3. Are you generally a private person? How do you feel about your partner sharing personal information about your relationship with friends and/or family?

4. If/when you have children, how much time do you believe children should spend with grandparents and other extended family? What role should in-laws play in your family life?

5. If there is a disagreement between you and your in-laws, whose role do you think it is to confront the issue? Should you always stand together as a couple when it comes to issues with the in-laws? Will loyalty to parents or siblings get in the way?

6. Are there cultural differences in your families that might cause problems? How much family togetherness is desired and expected? Should extended family be involved in helping to raise your children? At what point does involvement become interference?

7. How do families figure into holidays and other special occasions? Do you want your families included any time you have a party, or only for certain celebrations? Do you prefer to socialize separately with friends and family, or with everyone all together?

Ask these questions of one another and discuss your respective answers. As dating progresses toward a committed relationship, it will make for a more interesting courtship, revealing layers below the surface to help you build a healthier, lasting intimate bond.

Chapter Six

Sex and Gender-Role Issues

This chapter is really about how traditional or contemporary you want your relationship to be. More people are waiting longer to get married or enter a committed relationship than ever before in the history of mankind. Because of this rise in the average age of matrimony or commitment, individuals have more years to enjoy a degree of autonomy. Once experienced, the freedom of youthful independence is hard to give up. In modern, western cultures, the days of moving directly from a parent's home to the marital home are almost completely gone.

According to the Shriver report (2009), women make up half of the workforce in the United States. In four out of every five American families, both parents work outside the home, sharing responsibilities for finances. Obviously, with mom working outside the home, household and childrearing duties need to be discussed.

When you consciously split financial, household and childrearing responsibilities, whether based on traditional gender roles, ability, or any other criteria, you know where you stand. When you each clearly see/know where and how you fit into your surroundings, your home's day to day tasks have a greater chance of running smoothly. It's the silent assumptions we make that cause trouble. There are often quiet little unspoken truces that gloss over deeper disagreements. This may seem initially like a simple defense, an attempt to avoid dwelling on unpleasant details; but in time it fuels resentment in the relationship. It's best to deal with gender roles at the beginning of your partnership, making sure to agree or disagree as openly as possible.

Larry & Irene's Story

Sometimes gender conflicts are really about control issues. They can present as financial disagreements or a stand-off concerning sex, or any of a dozen other things. When Larry lost his job, Irene went to work. This disrupted a long-standing division of responsibilities along traditional gender lines.

When Irene first got her job, Larry was grateful to have the bills covered, and he actually took some pride in pitching in around the house, helping to shuttle their two children between school and their various activities. It turned out that Irene excelled at her job, and it wasn't long before she held a senior position in her firm.

When Larry found another job, they both agreed that Irene's income was important to their finances. Her salary helped them save for retirement, plan ahead for their children's education and look forward to family vacations. Plus, Irene really liked her job.

Larry hadn't counted on Irene enjoying work so much. He'd assumed that once he got back to work again, his position would take priority over Irene's. He had grudgingly agreed with Irene on a fair way to share household and childrearing tasks, but when she was promoted to an executive position, Larry grew more resentful. His anger came out in disparaging remarks about Irene's job, or snipes about her inability to attend to their children's needs. This cut Irene to the core, as she herself had ambivalent feelings about not being constantly available to the children, as she'd always been before.

Through the course of therapy, Larry came to understand how much he had appreciated Irene in the traditional role of wife and mother. At the same time, Irene came to understand that she didn't have to feel guilty that her role in the family had changed. Over time, they began to relate to each other in a new, more open and mature way, no longer programmed by former ideas of unconscious gender roles.

Irene learned more about self-determination and autonomy. She also made an effort to better understand the traditional core male values Larry embraced. At the same time, Larry grew to recognize and respect the traditional female instinct for care-giving. As they gained better understanding of themselves and each other, the experience deepened their relationship.

Biology plays a role here, to some extent. It is of course the woman who gives birth, which is significant. Beyond that, gender seems largely to be a product of the environment one is raised in. We are all raised within a broad social matrix of gender expectations; many of which are unconscious and taken for granted.

Men are socialized to hide emotion; falling short on showing empathy or responding to nonverbal cues. Women, on the other hand, tend to reply on empathy and nonverbal cues rather than direct, distinct communication. Women tend to discuss their wishes or needs as questions rather than statements of desire, which men are likely to regard as optional consider- ations. When a woman implies or intends a message that a man simply doesn't pick up on, the barrier is real and both parties are equally to blame. It's best to be specific and explicit when communicating with the opposite sex. We are wired differ- ently; we think differently. Without being direct and honest at all times, we open ourselves and those we love to unnecessary anguish.

So, are "traditional" roles of husband and wife falling into the past? Not necessarily. It depends mostly on the beliefs and values of each couple. There are spouses who are happy to embrace traditional gender roles once they are married; perhaps it's how they were raised and it worked well for their parents, or because of religious beliefs, or simply because a tra- ditional division of responsibilities suits them.

In a traditional marriage, the husband is the breadwinner while the wife maintains the home and takes care of the children. The man handles the money and the wife is given a budget to use for family shopping. Investments and long-term retirement planning are usually the man's responsibilities. There are clear divisions of labor between "man's work" (income earning, trash removal, autumn leaves, car maintenance, light-bulb changing, bug kill- ing) and "woman's work" (grocery shopping, primary parenting, food and meal prep, household cleaning and operations, laundry, mommy taxi, entertaining, holidays and celebrations, gift buying for family and friends, etc.).

If the two of you decide that a traditional configuration works well for you, by all means, follow it, but be sure you agree on the details. There is no particular model that you are required to emulate. What matters is to craft the balance that is fair in your home, and brings your family together instead of splitting it apart.

Part of agreeing to details of divided responsibility is to understand what they entail. Some fathers wouldn't know how to change a diaper if their life depended on it. Those dads never had to learn, because presumably everyone was happy with it that way. In other families, I've seen first-hand when a baby is screaming to be changed while two toddlers are also clamoring for Mom's attention, all as Dad watches a football game!

This is not to say that these dads don't care or aren't wonderful fathers . It's simply that the moment to moment role of meeting children's demands still belongs to the mom in many households. This dynamic is carried on from previous generations, or it can change for a more modern model, depending upon what you both want for your family. The roles that you define early in your relationship will be quickly and easily adopted or even exploited by children. Be careful what you wish for!

In reality, most marriages today are more egalitarian. This means that before children come along, both partners work outside the home. When children arrive, either or both parents may cut back on working hours in order to take care of the little ones. Many couples arrange babysitting or daycare to help maintain family income levels without neglecting the children, but the cost of help can sometimes overshadow the income it enables. Life and parenting are a tough balancing act, to be sure. Still today in many cases, mom quits her job to stay at home, at least until the children are older and in school full-time.

If you and your spouse decide together that mom will stay home with children after she's been out in the working world for years, discuss what you will each do to make sure she still gets intellectual stimulation. The transition from being a professional with an income to an at-home parent can be very difficult. It isn't easy to switch from being in a world of adults all day, every day, to spending all waking hours in the land of diapers and feedings.

When women work outside the home as most do today, they still end up doing a vast majority of the household chores. This is not because they married bad men, but because of how easy it is to settle into traditional roles, even in modern families. It is essential to discuss all the things that go into making a household run smoothly, and how each partner will contribute.

Whereas many couples clearly discuss a desire (or lack of desire) for children, they may never have discussed how they would handle raising children once they arrive. Many people (both male and female) feel strongly that certain gender-roles should be maintained, but may not think to talk about it with their partner. Unfortunately, it isn't safe to assume that they feel the same.

Chapter Six: Sex and Gender-Role Issues

Ideas about gender-specific roles can create dangerous resent-ment if not properly discussed. Some people come from homes that were clearly gender-role specific. Mom took care of the inside of the home, while dad took care of the outside.

> *"Sometimes I wonder if men and women really suit each other. Perhaps they should live next door, and just visit now and then."*
> *Katherine Hepburn*

When either partner in a relationship has specific ideas about who should do what, misunderstanding and arguments can result. There are many people who still believe that a woman should do all the laundry, cleaning, cooking and shopping. Those same people may feel adamant that mowing grass is man's work.

What if the man of the house loves to cook and the woman is an avid gardener? Traditional gender roles may not work for this couple. In a relationship, we may very well understand our partner's likes, dislikes and interests, but it's amazing how often people assume that once marriage is in place, the other partner will become miraculously flexible. Be careful, because this is NOT always the case!

In most families today, the lines have been blurred between "male jobs" and "female jobs." Instead, the division of labor is usually based on a combination of variables such as time, skill, inclination and interest. Some couples negotiate these things in a way that feels very fair and appropriate to both parties. The balance of responsibility comes naturally to them and they move through life without the bits of anger that can build up over time. However, other couples sometimes resent what they see as a very uneven balance of chores. In these cases, it is usually the woman who feels overburdened and the man who feels constantly nagged.

What will work best for you? The only answer is to talk about all the chores involved in maintaining a household; cooking, cleaning, laundry, dishes (and emptying the dishwasher), feeding and walking a dog, grocery shopping, hanging pictures, home repairs, lawn and garden tasks, car maintenance, and yes – even taking out the garbage. Especially when both partners work full-time outside the home, household chores must be shared. If you don't communicate to divide chores fairly, you leave plenty of room for resentment to fester.

Look at marriage through the lens of a business. If the business of marriage is to run your household, there are many things that contribute to its smooth function. In addition to the day to day chores listed above, there is also keeping accurate financial records, preparing taxes, planning vacations, shoveling snow (if applicable), etc. The list of responsibilities in life is endless, and that is before special crises or needs arise. When roles are not clearly defined and tasks are not assigned, it's easy for a ball to drop and cause conflict. When there are no clean clothes on a Monday morning, or someone slips on ice because the walk wasn't shoveled, or a child gets hurt because a loose step wasn't repaired, you are headed for trouble.

Yes, chores are dull. Talking about them might sound dull too, but it is well worth the investment of time. List various chores and how often you each expect them to get done. Determine which chores are priorities when time is short. When you each have common expectations, you can both feel the success of a home that runs like a well-oiled machine.

If your husband is picky about the car's appearance, then keeping it clean should probably be his job. Perhaps one partner hates doing laundry, but doesn't mind washing dishes. These are the starting points for healthy compromise. If you both thoroughly despise mowing the lawn, factor some money into your budget to hire an outside contractor, or alternate mowing to share that chore. Another option is to handle yard work together, as a team. This usually makes it go faster, and may even end up being a fun way to spend time together. Bottom line: Planning ahead with realistic and fair expectations helps keep all systems running smoothly.

There is nothing wrong with embracing traditional gender-roles, and there's nothing in any way wrong with rejecting them. The only thing that matters is that you examine, reveal and negotiate your preferences *before* you're in a situation that can't be reversed.

Figure out a way to share your schedules and communicate about special circumstances, like a meeting with your child's teacher, so you can figure out who will attend and what additional tasks might need to be done. When you agree about who will do what, write it down and post it somewhere you'll both be able to see it. If your partner volunteers to do something, then leave it at that; don't nag. If the chore doesn't get accomplished, bring it up for discussion in a calm manner, rather than in the heat of an angry moment. Remember, winning is when you are happy together, not when you "win" while your partner "loses."

If you are the one being nagged, accept that you play a part in creating stress for your spouse. If you are the one nagging, you may have trust issues that go beyond the matter at hand. The more honest you are with yourself, the more honest you'll be with your partner.

If one of you consistently fails to follow through on what was promised, try to uncover what the problem might be. Perhaps there is an underlying issue. Sometimes in a traditional marriage, the provider feels that working long hours (to earn extra money for the family) justifies skipping household chores. Maybe it does, but this needs to be a conscious and mutual decision, not based on assumptions about gender roles. When one partner doesn't do their chores, those chores don't go away. They are still there for one of you to do.

If you have drastically different ideas about what chores need to be done and what level of cleanliness needs to be maintained, or if you both decide that other obligations are higher priorities than taking care of your home, I suggest trying to afford and hire housekeeping help. It may comfort you to know that there is an entire industry devoted to helping people organize their homes more efficiently.

"Political promises are much like marriage vows;
they are made at the beginning of the relationship between
candidate and voter, but quickly forgotten."
Dick Gregory

It's fairly common to hear that men have a hard time admitting to emotional needs, but women are conditioned while growing up to be sensitive and accommodating to the needs of others. Although women can also have trouble identifying their own needs, they are often more able to seek help or emotional connection. According to psychiatrist Matina Horner, some women may actually fear success and autonomy because they worry it will mean disconnection from loved ones.

For many women, money equals love. Being taken care of is a part of a love partnership, and if a woman provides for herself financially, she may fear that means she doesn't need a man to care for her. In this way her emotional need (real and reasonable) is tied together with financial need. These can be hard issues to unravel, but it's important to probe your deepest attitudes about gender-roles to find out what's at stake for you.

There are frequently misunderstandings between the sexes about strength and weakness. People have pre-conceived notions about crying. Both men and women sometimes view crying as a sign of weakness. However, as women are often discouraged from showing anger, sometimes crying is their involuntary way of expressing rage or disappointment, as well as sadness. Although women may fear or even resent angry outbursts, for men such outbursts can be a default, One Size Fits All reaction to any unpleasant situation.

Gender differences present the most fundamental obstacles between men and women, and it's interesting to give them some thought. Be mindful, however, that the most important test of any relationship comes from how you relate to each other as two human beings shaping a life together.

Patty & Rob's Story

Patty and Rob dated for eight years before getting married. They had lived together for most of those years and were completely clear when it came to their "gender roles" around the home. Essentially, there were none. Anything that had to be done was handled by whomever was available to do it. It seemed for eight years that things were working out perfectly, until one day brought a surprise - Patty found herself pregnant with twins.

Unplanned and unexpected, the couple faced the pregnancy together. At first it appeared that things would keep rolling along as usual. Once the babies were born, however, things changed drastically. Since daycare was too costly for twins, Patty reluctantly decided to stay home with them. As soon as Patty became an at-home Mom, Rob's entire attitude changed.

Suddenly, Rob was the sole breadwinner. He expected a hot dinner on the table in the evening and ignored household duties like laundry and cleaning. Even worse, since Patty was with the twins all day, he simply let her take over parenting duties as well. By the time the twins were two, Patty was exhausted and fed up with doing everything by herself. Rob had become presumptuous and left her to handle everything.

When they ended up in my office, Rob and Patty were on the brink of divorce. Rob had grown up with a stay-at-home mom who had done everything in their household. He always assumed that his mom had liked it that way. His dad had worked during the week and spent time with the children on weekends, but the younger children were always left to their mother. Rob simply assumed that was how life should be.

> *"I have yet to hear a man ask for advice on how to combine marriage and a career."*
> Gloria Stinem

Patty, on the other hand, felt like she was forced to give up her career to become a housewife - something she was not fond of. Actually, she'd never wanted children and certainly did not want to carry all the responsibility alone. When discussion opened up between them in our sessions, Rob and Patty's issues were mostly about carrying on gender-specific roles from an earlier generation.

Neither spouse had meant to hurt the other. Rob had the impression that Patty had everything under control, and would resent his help or intervention at home. He could remember his mother complaining about the way his dad did things like laundry or dishes, and didn't want his wife to resent his meddling in her domain that way. Once he learned that Patty was unhappy and actually wanted help for a healthier balance, we were on our way to finding their best compromise.

In this case, Rob and Patty made a chart of household responsibilities and split them down the middle. This included responsibilities related to the children. Patty continued to stay at home, but Saturdays became her day to go out and do anything that she wanted for herself. As a result of having responsibility for the twins one day each week, Rob quickly grew to appreciate all the hard work Patty did with their kids and around their home.

It's easy to fall into traditional roles when modern schedules are so jam-packed. A wife may act more like a mother or organizer, taking care of day to day household tasks. A husband may feel justified for staying longer hours at work, especially if he is the sole or primary source of income. Try to remember the people you are beneath the roles you play. Make time to spend together, even if you have to build it into your schedule. Reconnect as people with hopes, dreams and interests beyond daily work or parenting. This way you will help bring order to your life in a way that suits you both, so you can each look forward to the same life as you build it together. However you divide responsibilities, the goal is to remain partners in your relationship rather than people in charge of separate realms.

Debbie & Sam's Story

Gender issues can often get mixed up with issues about control - sometimes even issues about the remote control! Before Debbie and Sam moved in together, Debbie rarely even watched TV; but she did enjoy hanging out with Sam and watching TV with him. At least, she did at first.

In the beginning, they both liked watching movies and sci-fi TV series. Then, as time went on, Debbie found herself resenting the way Sam assumed control of the TV remote *every single time*. He would decide what they'd watch for both of them. He had a habit of clicking away from a program they were both watching as soon as he became impatient or wanted to channel-surf. It annoyed Debbie that Sam often clicked the TV on the moment he came home from work, without even saying hello first.

Worst of all though, was Sam's obsession with sports. He would watch anything that had to do with sports; not only games and special events, but interviews, programs about equipment, biographies on the players, etc. Sometimes Sam would settle on a sporting event or program that Debbie knew he didn't even care about. She started to nag him about his TV watching, and finally complained so much about the time Sam spent watching sports, that he bought her a TV for the bedroom so she could watch whatever she wanted.

A new TV was SO not the point! Debbie understood Sam being a sports fan and wanting to watch certain events, games or programs throughout each season. She only believed it was unfair that Sam dominated all of their time with his TV choices, almost acting as if she wasn't there. While they didn't have to agree on every program all the time, splitting off to separate rooms wasn't the "solution" she had in mind.

Debbie gave it a try, but felt more and more that they were building separate lives, mostly dictated by what was on TV. And, it was getting worse. With a TV in the bedroom, Sam brought some of the same domineering TV habits to bed. Debbie was disturbed enough to schedule a therapy session.

For the most part, Sam hadn't given TV viewing much thought. For him, it was a way to unwind and zone out. Debbie thought a little of that was fine, but for her there was too much zoning out going on, and it was affecting their relationship.

In an article, "Couples Watching Television: Gender, Power, and the Remote Control," Family Studies Professor Alexis J. Walker demonstrates the way gender and control issues creep into even seemingly innocuous everyday situations, such as who controls the TV remote control.

Television watching can become a battleground for unconscious gender stereotypes, with men most often asserting control over the remote, to dominate what is viewed. Meanwhile, women are going about making and cleaning up after dinner, supervising homework, bathing and getting children ready for bed. This further entrenches stereotypical gender roles, and a division of power along traditional lines.

Debbie and Sam were surprised to learn that they were far from alone in dealing with this issue. After talking it over, they decided on some compromises: they agreed to only watch TV at certain times, unless they wanted to watch a particular program or unique event. Sam picked his three favorite sports and limited his viewing to two games on weekends; except when one of his favorite teams made it to end-of-season playoffs. Debbie understood his being a fan with special interest in particular teams, and was happy to be flexible for the playoffs. She also agreed to learn about one sport- she'd always wanted to follow baseball- so they could watch that sport together. Sam filled her in on the rules and player statistics for baseball, and they both happily enjoyed sharing this activity - it even led to new time spent together. Sam knew that he could now always count on Debbie to see a live baseball game with him. When he watched his other sports, Debbie worked on knitting projects.

They agreed to alternate who controlled the remote, and to record any show the other person would miss. They also got rid of the bedroom TV, saving the bedroom for sleep and other, more important things...

There were still some areas of friction, here and there. Genuine compromise takes time and a bit of giving on both sides, but they became more sensitive to each other's needs - not only about TV, but about other things as well. For instance, Debbie had always left it to Sam to decide where they were going out for dinner, or what movie they were going to see. When she found out that Sam didn't always want to be the one making decisions, they began to alternate who made those choices as well.

Two people coming together doesn't (or shouldn't) mean that the original individuals disappear. The idea is that you both care for and appreciate each other enough to remain individuals as you build a life together. Not every moment will be harmony, but when you can step back and truly hear your partner, then take an honest look in the mirror and move together toward a middle ground, you are on your way to a divorce-proof marriage.

Harrison and Leah's Story

TV is only one example of gender control. There is also, of course, the issue of sexual compatibility. One couple was very much in love but they had extremely different libidos. Harrison was happy with having sex about once a month, but Leah wanted sex at least once a day, preferably twice. Although they've been married for twenty years, sexual frequency was still an issue for them.

Leah felt rejected. She wondered if Harrison was involved with someone else. In turn, Harrison often felt defensive, even though he was doing nothing wrong. When they did have sex, he didn't enjoy it much, because he felt like he was being pressured to perform. Over time, they grew further and further apart because the marital bed became a place of awkwardness and resentment, instead of rest and pleasure.

When Leah and Harrison came to me, we first discussed the messages they had each received about sex from their parents when they were growing up. Both seemed to have healthy sexual attitudes. I suggested that Harrison discuss his low libido with his physician. Tests were run, and the results showed low testosterone levels. This was a relief for both of them.

The physician encouraged first trying natural supplements, and soon Harrison was finding interest in sex at least a couple of times a week. Interestingly, this was plenty for Leah. Once she was no longer feeling rejected, she no longer needed or craved daily intercourse.

As a couple is dating and during the honeymoon period, lovers experience a heightened level of sexual attraction. Over time however, life returns to "normal," with all the responsibilities of work, household, family, finances, etc. This can sometimes drain sexual energy away. Diminished or varying desires for sex can affect partners very differently, and it should be talked about. One of the most common complaints of married people is lack of sex, which is not always due to a lack of wanting sex, but a lack of time or energy for sex.

With other couples, a frequent complaint is HOW they have sex. Some people (usually women) are uncomfortable with their bodies or generally shy. They will only have sex at night with the lights out, in the missionary position. Other lovers want to see their partner's body and are less inhibited. They enjoy trying different positions and lovemaking techniques. Experimenting can be a sensitive line to walk, when trying to introduce a partner to new possibilities while ensuring that they feel safe and comfortable.

At some point, a few sessions with a therapist might be helpful for couples struggling with sexual differences. It's important to discuss even the most sensitive subjects to be sure you can reach a mutually satisfying compromise. Every couple should also realize that time, age, children and health considerations may change sexual habits.

Bill & Sue's Story

Bill and Sue had an active and healthy sex life while they were dating and engaged. They seemed to have compatible sex drives and a thriving intimate life was important to both of them. After marriage, things began to slow down a bit. They soon had children, and Bill started to sense that sex was no longer a priority for Sue. He was angry and hurt, believing that the lack of intimacy from Sue was a direct result of something she felt about him.

Sue would try to explain that she was simply exhausted and constantly busy; that nursing and keeping up with young children seemed to rob her of her sex drive. In addition, motherhood had changed her. She almost felt guilty about having sexual urges. Sue had grown up in a very conservative home. Her mother had never been the least bit 'sexy' or forward.

The more Bill pushed the issue, the more Sue pulled away. Finally, after a few years, Bill could take no more rejection and ended up having an affair. When Sue found out, Bill was indignant and accusatory. He had needs and felt that his wife should have met them. Fortunately, they came to my office.

In the early years, Sue and Bill hadn't discussed their sex lives because they were always compatible. Life tends to bring changes over time, and as circumstances occurred and Sue's priorities shifted, sex basically dropped off of her list of things "to-do." This is unfortunately common in marriage. Bill expected Sue to know how he felt, and Sue couldn't understand why Bill wasn't more compassionate. What Sue didn't realize was that to Bill, sex was a major factor in his connection to his wife. He fiercely believed that a happy marriage means having sex several times a week.

Sue and Bill are still in counseling; trying to heal from Bill's affair and learning to make time for each other as husband and wife again. Their success still remains to be seen.

Too many people are afraid to discuss sex with their partner. This sadly results in many spouses looking outside their marriage for satisfaction. Sex becomes routine and sometimes even feels like a chore. Because they don't discuss sex, many couples live their lives together never fully satisfying each other, until sex is no longer a part of their relationship at all. If sex is painful, let your partner know, so you can begin to resolve the problem. If you have a fantasy, share it with your lover. Each particular desire may not be something he/she is interested in, but when you can both reveal what excites you, you will connect in a new and passionate way that will keep your sex life intimate and enticing.

If you're afraid to mention a problem, do it anyway! You're better off learning now to communicate with each other. It will help you negotiate your way through problems for the duration of your relationship. If your partner is convinced that a given issue is your problem only and you need to solve it alone, this is a big clue that communication is only going to get more difficult down the line.

Keep a spark in your love with the pleasure of being close. Make time to connect with each other every day. Set aside ten minutes in your schedule, if that's what you have to do. It will be worth it. Little gestures (like a hug as your partner walks by, or holding hands at the movies) go a long way toward nurturing harmony between you. You may no longer have the time or money for a weekend at Niagara Falls, but it costs nothing to write a little love note.

Intimacy isn't only about sex. It's about deeply knowing, accepting and appreciating your partner; and feeling that you are known, accepted and appreciated for being yourself. There are all sorts of tiny ways to stay in touch with the intimate connection between you. When you find and develop your own list of loving habits, a surprising thing happens - you keep finding new reasons to love your partner, and you feel even more loved in return.

> *"Being deeply loved by someone gives you strength, while loving someone deeply gives you courage."*
> *Lao Tzu*

Questions about Sex & Gender-Role Issues

As always, I recommend that each of you devote some private, individual time to read and consider these questions. Try to reveal your own answers and desires to yourself, before addressing them with your partner. You can only be fair and truly attentive as a lover when you know yourself first.

1. Think about your parents. What roles did they play in your childhood home? Do you agree or disagree with those roles and why? When you marry, what is it you envision your partner vs. yourself doing around the home, for/with the children, etc.?

2. Do you feel strongly that any work, chore or activity is strictly decided by gender? If so, which ones and why?

3. If either partner must one day decide to stay at home, whom do you believe it should it be and why?

4. Think about the terms traditional vs. non-traditional. Define them in your own words as they relate to a marriage commitment.

5. Consider your current sexual relationship. What's great about it and/or what do you feel could or should be improved?

6. In your opinion, how often should a husband & wife engage in sexual intimacy? How would you feel if you were forced to go several months without sex?

How would you feel if you were expected to have sex several times each week?

7. How comfortable are you discussing sex or sexual issues with your partner? Are there issues that you consider taboo? Does pornography have a place in your sex life? Is it acceptable for either of you to enjoy it alone? If you found your lover watching an adult film, would you take off your clothes and join him/her, or quietly leave the room feeling embarrassed and insecure?

This is not about judging right or wrong. The goal of these essential conversations is to know yourself on a deeper level so you can best find, attract and KEEP the perfect partner for you.

Chapter Seven

Communication and Handling Disagreements

"All married couples should learn the art of battle as they should learn the art of making love. Good battle is objective and honest – never vicious or cruel. Good battle is healthy and constructive, and brings to a marriage the principle of equal partnership."
Ann Landers

imagine that if you and your partner have made it this far in the book, you have found some areas of disagreement. Good! Your ability to handle disagreements may be the most important skill you will need in your relationship.

It has often been said, "Don't sweat the small stuff." Well, maybe it's important to recognize that almost all of life is small stuff. The things we argue about most often are inconsequential in the bigger scheme of life. When you feel bothered by something petty, ask yourself: "will this really matter a month (or a year) from now?" If your answer is NO, it's probably not worth worrying about.

On the other hand, don't allow a significant conflict to continue without being addressed. This is a recipe for certain resentment down the line. Many people would rather sulk than admit being wrong, but "I'm sorry," are two of the most powerful and healing words you can say to another person; especially your partner, in times of conflict. Don't be afraid to be the first person to apologize. Remember, love isn't a contest. The only way you win is when you're both happy together.

Alex & Barbara's Story

Alex and Barbara are a lesbian couple who have been in a committed relationship for several years. They have both been competitive athletes and saw every interaction as a challenge to be won or lost. They literally kept score! "She was 15 minutes late getting home last night, so I'm going to be 20 minutes late tonight, just to show her." Or, "she only cooked dinner twice last week and I cooked four times. I'm not cooking tonight, even if we don't eat at all." When they argued, even about something trivial, it always escalated into a loud and ugly exchange because each had to have the last word.

When I suggested that they respond to each other with, "I disagree with you, but that's okay. You're entitled to your opinion…." they both looked at me as if I were from another planet. Their expressions simultaneously said, "How can you win doing THAT?" I suggested that most of their arguments were, in fact, just a difference of opinion, not something that really mattered to the relationship in the bigger scheme of things. *Agreeing to disagree just might be the most important skill to learn in building strong relationships.* And by the way, this applies to ALL relationships, not just the romantic variety.

Remembering that love is not a contest, let's review some communication tools that help couples work through difficulties. It's been said that we were each given two ears and one mouth because they were meant to be used proportionally. LISTENING is essential to healthy, effective communication.

Active listening means making sure you understand what the other person is saying. Paraphrasing is useful: "If I understand you correctly, what you're really saying is that you don't like going out with Sarah and Josh because he's always trying to one-up you. I can understand how you might get that impression." You might continue by saying, "I always thought Josh felt less successful than you and he was being overly defensive."

Notice that the speaker first acknowledged hearing what her partner said, and instead of saying "you're wrong," she simply posed another possibility. She did this by using what are called "I messages." She owned her own thoughts about the situation without saying he was off base. By using "I," she was essentially saying that while she had a different perspective, she could also understand his point of view. This way, no one loses.

Be sure the time you've picked to talk is good for both of you. If you try to have a meaningful discussion as your partner is trying to get out the door for work in the morning, chances are you won't get a desired response, and you'll both be left feeling disappointed and letdown. While you work to improve your listening skills, be mindful of behaviors that may make it hard to hear what you're saying. Timing is important for communication to be productive and to keep stress is at a minimum.

Be as concise as possible. Don't monopolize the conversation. Don't lecture or pontificate; this might sound like you're talking down to your partner. The intent is to create a dialogue. Give your partner a chance to speak or ask questions, or clarify a statement you've made. If you've said hurtful or intimidating things in the past, be aware that your partner may be bracing for this kind of abusive behavior rather than giving you undivided attention. Only time and consistency will change this. When you stop saying mean or disrespectful things, you'll find your partner much more receptive to what you are trying to get across.

Say what you mean as directly and honestly as you can. If your partner senses that what you're saying is not expressing your true message, especially if this has been an issue before, you can be sure you're not going to get your spouse's full attention. Acknowledge times in the past when you have been indirect or even manipulative in conversations. Tell the truth as soon as you know it yourself, and keep honesty a priority in your relationship at all times.

Avoid using sweeping generalizations, especially when describing your spouse's behavior. Be specific when describing a grievance. Don't say things like "you always" or, "you never," because your partner may automatically tune out . Keep in mind that no one will listen to a constant barrage of nagging and whining. Would you? If you want your mate to be a better listener, practice being a better listener yourself. Be prepared, though, for occasional differences of opinion, and remember that it's not the end of the world.

At the risk of sounding redundant, I can't stress enough how very important it is to take time to A) *know*, and B) *own* your feelings. Take responsibility for the perspectives you bring to the relationship. Otherwise you become a victim, and the other person, a perpetrator. Your lover is not supposed to be an adversary!

As soon as you say, "YOU make me so angry," you have become a victim by giving the other person power over your feelings. This naturally puts your partner on the defensive, which doesn't help. When a sentence begins with "You," it's like pointing a verbal finger. What is a natural defensive response? To either push back, or figuratively retreat. Neither is constructive behavior, and neither leads to problem resolution. If your goals are peace, harmony and affection, consider that nagging and accusing your spouse only fans flames of fury, not flames of passion.

Over and over in my practice, I've heard people say "She made me so angry," or "He totally embarrassed me." I consistently point out that they're victims giving away power over their feelings and in fact, these statements are inaccurate. No one MAKES you feel a certain way.

Here is an example I often use in my practice:

> *Imagine for a minute that you're at a cocktail party where you know no one. You've just walked in, and you observe the following scene: A man is very drunk and dancing around with a lampshade on his head. As you look around the room, you see various responses to*

his behavior. Some people are laughing and think it's hysterical – he's the life of the party. Others think he's obnoxious and disgusting. The host is worried that there might be a fight over car keys at the end of the evening; and the man's wife would like to crawl under the floor, she's so embarrassed.

Which emotion is the man responsible for? Which way did he make the observers feel? Of course he did not make anyone feel any particular way. Each person responded to him based on their own history and their relationship (or lack of relationship) to him.

Every moment of our lives, we are observing and experiencing. Each experience and human exchange becomes a part of our data bank. We each have a unique data bank because no two people have identical experiences.

When we see, hear, smell, taste or touch something new, it is filtered through our existing data bank. How we respond emo-tionally to each experience depends in large part on our unique set of filters. Thus, when we see different people with a range of responses to the drunken party guest – each observer is respond-ing through their own set of filters. Bottom line: Don't ever give your power away by blaming someone else for your feelings!

People are often comfortable expressing their thoughts and opinions, but much less willing to reveal or share feelings. This is worth mentioning and working on, because sharing feelings is an essential part of developing intimacy, and as any relationship matures, the ability to communicate your feelings will be crucial to solving problems.

Some people may have trouble sharing feelings because they haven't consciously separated their thoughts (information) from their emotions (sensitivities). Once you pass Step 1 – to recognize and own your emotions, the next step is 2 – being able to communicate them. If you need help, keep a list of basic emotions (angry, sad, happy, afraid, etc.) someplace handy. This list will help you quickly and easily identify your own emotions as life rolls forward.

You can use a list of adverbs to describe how you're feeling to your partner. Convey intensity in your voice, your eyes and your body language. When you add up the powerful communication tools we all naturally have, it's a wonder that anyone has to guess at what we mean to say. If you have trouble communicating verbally or physically, it may be easier to write down what you need to say, so your partner can read it.

Feelings are nothing to be afraid of. They come and go. They're neither right nor wrong. How you handle your emotions is what matters. It's OK to express anger, but not OK to hit your partner (or anyone else!). Physical violence is always crossing a line. Refrain from judging yourself or your spouse. Encourage openness, safety and comfort when your partner has something difficult to express.

Some couples disagree when an important decision must be made. For example, maybe one wants to accept a new job in a different city, but the other doesn't want to move. Obviously, something has to give. In a situation like this, it may be best to start with a list of pros and cons, then proceed with a brainstorm session to figure out how to maximize the pros and minimize the cons.

When evaluating pros and cons of any big decision, try to be as specific as possible. The more practically you consider implications to daily life, the more accurately you can make a wise choice.

What is really to be gained from the move? Is the new job more money? Does the title offer prestige? Is it a once-in-a-lifetime challenge and fulfilling career opportunity? Are there other ways of accomplishing the same goal without selling the current home? Does it mean moving away from family and friends? Will it require the children to change schools? Is there a way to make the move more palatable?

Once you list all the questions, challenges, pros and cons, you can start to negotiate a healthy compromise. (If you'll go along with me on the move, I promise you can pick the new house).

Be creative. Sleep on it. Brainstorm some more. Even in the most seemingly black and white situations, there is usually room for some flexibility. If you really reach a brick wall, consult a therapist, mediator, or some other objective, disinterested and well respected third party to help you make your decision.

What if you tend to disagree about smaller things and it feels like "he/she always gets his/her way." Whether it comes to what movie you'll see, where you go to dinner, or where you'll go on vacation, it's amazing how often these little things turn into big arguments. Try to remember again that it's not a contest; it won't matter a year from now.

If/when tempers flare, take time out. This doesn't mean running away from the problem, but talking it through an hour later or the next day won't usually make or break a situation. Don't put it off for too long, and don't ignore it. Just recognize that a heated argument rarely solves anything, and it's best to take time to cool off and regain some perspective.

If, after the cooling off period, a decision still cannot be reached, you might want to have a strategy. One obvious option is to simply take turns. If you had your way last time, it's your partner's turn this time. Other long standing problem-solving tactics are: Flip a coin. Draw straws. Rock, paper, scissor (two out of three!). It really doesn't matter how you make decisions on these relatively unimportant issues. What counts is that you acknowledge differing desires and resolve each conflict in a fair way. When you each bend a little, you each get your way about half the time, so neither of you are likely to feel cheated or over-compromised.

Bruce & Jane's Story

Bruce & Jane had been married for 24 years. They managed throughout their marriage to disagree, but never agreed on how to argue or negotiate solutions. Bruce always reacted to disagreement, arguments or discussions with a defensive attitude and a raised voice, in order to get his point across. Jane, although once quite opinionated, began early in the relationship to keep quiet or shut down. Sometimes Jane chose not to bring things up at all, to avoid confrontation and Bruce's volatile temper.

Jane didn't think she would ever get Bruce to see her point of view, so there was no point to discussing certain things. Over time, little things like where to go for dinner or what to watch on TV were always decided by Bruce. Jane relinquished any control by simply remaining silent. As the years wore on, this unhealthy pattern Jane had created for herself began to breed a deep resentment.

When Jane suddenly announced one day that their marriage was over, Bruce was truly shocked. He didn't understand, couldn't understand, because Jane had never seemed unhappy. According to him, they never argued or disagreed. What could be so wrong?

Jane saw their marriage very differently. She had grown up in a dysfunctional home with a raging mother, and had decided long ago that she would not be an angry person. Instead, she simply shut down. In essence, Jane had never learned to deal with any relationship problems because she went along with whatever Bruce wanted in order to keep the peace.

Bruce, in his defense, may have perhaps been a bit overbearing, but never had a chance to understand what Jane was feeling. Because Jane silently went along with whatever he wanted, Bruce had no idea that there was any problem. In this situation, the relationship was too far gone to save. Jane had felt oppressed and walked on by Bruce. She was beyond apology or compromise. Sadly, this was not Bruce's fault. If someone doesn't know how you feel because you choose to not tell them, there is nothing that you can do about the outcome.

We owe it to our loved ones to use our voice and share our opinions, whether we get our way or not. It is imperative for life partners to know where their spouses stand, so you can each remain true to yourselves while living with, and for, one another. There is an old phrase that says you have to "stand for something or you will fall for anything." In this marriage, Jane fell for a life that was decided by someone else and she caused herself to feel unheard and unimportant.

Make a deal to always talk to each other about family issues, even difficult matters that you'd rather not bring up. Part of that deal must be a commitment to refrain from ever using this trust against each other, or repeating a confidence in anger at a later date. Problems simply don't get solved that way. When a couple decides to stop talking about important issues, secrets get kept, resentment builds, and previously loving partners drift apart. Create rules in your relationship to keep from hurting each other, and in time, as trust between you grows, the bond you share will be stronger.

In a marriage or long-term relationship, dealing with life's issues together is essential. No life is without struggle or disagreement. The trick is finding something that works for both partners and allows each to be heard. Unfortuantely, if an unwelcome or offensive behavior continues for too long, like in the case with Bruce and Jane, there is sometimes no turning back.

We all may know one or two of those couples who argue about *everything*, not only the subject at hand. They "gunnysack" – i.e. keep track of years' worth of small (or not so small) infractions, pulling old offenses out of the sack whenever they're upset with their partner. If either of you do this, cry "FOUL." Always keep an argument focused on the issue at hand. There is nothing you can do to change the past.

Other personal fouls that often occur during arguments are things like name calling ("you're just like your mother"), hitting below the belt (where one partner says something simply because they know it will hurt the other person), and so forth. These behaviors are immature, unfair, unnecessary, and do not create an environment conducive to problem solving, much less loving harmony.

While some people are comfortable with screaming and hostility, others inwardly cringe and shut down. Be sure that your approach is not shutting your partner down when you're trying to communicate or solve problems. It's about the two of you, so you both need to be involved. Also, remember that things said in anger can't be taken back. Think twice about a nasty remark in a heated moment, before you voice it out loud. Even in a time of conflict, you are speaking to the person you love. What purpose does it serve to hurt them?

There are classic bad habits that put a quick stop to effective communication. Don't think about what you're going to say while the other person is speaking. Focus on what they are saying and listen with your whole being. Be mindful that responding with anger and derision to a loved one may shut down all possibility of honest exchange, not only in the moment, but also in future discussions.

Here are some tips to bear in mind during arguments with a loved one: When speaking, try to frame your statements with positive rather than negative words. A hostile tone will only put your listener on the defensive. Be as clear as you can be; remember, your partner can't read your mind. Express your thoughts on thorny issues by conveying how you are being affected.

Keep blame out of it. State facts about how you feel when something occurs using your list of emotions, so your partner is less likely to feel blamed. State your response to a behavior that has upset you and the reason it upset you as: "I felt hurt when you that, because your opinion is important to me." Choose your words carefully, with compassion. Remember, the tone of your voice can either add friction or smooth it over. When you explain how you feel about your partner's behavior instead of placing blame, you'll be less likely to provoke an argument.

Concentrate on solving one specific problem that you've identified. Don't expand your discussion to include other issues, character flaws, or problems from the past. Put your creative minds to work generating ideas to solve the problem you face. Don't judge or dismiss any options; all ideas should be considered. Discuss alternatives and pinpoint a solution you can both agree to. Talk through possible obstacles to implementation. Though this will likely involve compromise, both parties will feel listened to, considered, empowered and trusted. Working through conflicts this way will bring you closer together and strengthen the bond between you.

Even though you may be stressed, take time to assess your partner's needs. Remember the importance of timing when it comes to discussing problems. A light, routine conversation about your day can also help relieve stress and is a good way to spend time together, unwinding for the evening.

Improving your ability to communicate takes a lot of practice, but the rewards are worth the effort, both immediately and down the line as your relationship evolves. Becoming better communicators will help you feel more connected to each other. Don't reserve communication only for problem solving!

By including regular "family" time in your weekly schedule, you can ensure that not too much time passes without you and your partner having a chance to catch up with your thoughts. Chat while walking together or doing chores. Hopefully, you feel free to talk about anything with your partner. Keeping the lines of communication open means your chances of solving problems are even better. Communication means not only saying what you mean in the clearest way, but making sure your message has been heard the way you intended. Respect your differences, and respect each other.

Questions about Handling Communication & Disagreements

1. How do you *honestly* feel about your partner's ability to deal with conflict? What could your partner do to make communication easier for both of you? Is there a point of compromise?

2. Look back through your life file to recall how disagreements were handled by your parents. How did their arguments make you feel? What do you want to do differently, or the same?

3. Can you think of (and agree on) a plan to handle disagreements and come to a compromise even when it's obvious that you won't agree? Consider some real life situations.

4. Look back over your relationship to date. Can you name three specific moments when you felt bad or resentful about how a problem was resolved? Why?

5. Describe your partner's communication style with you, and yours with your partner. Do either of you ever commit personal fouls?

In Conclusion

"For two people in a marriage to live together day after day is
unquestionably the one miracle the Vatican has overlooked."
Bill Cosby

All marriages are challenging at one time or another, but certain factors can particularly contribute to divorce: getting married very young, for instance; if one or both of you never completed your education; if you were raised in different faiths or if you came from a divorced family; if you're struggling financially.

If you are worried that your relationship is in trouble and you can't seem to resolve your differences, consider couples' counseling. The sooner you begin therapy after identifying a problem, the better your chance for peaceful and satisfactory resolution.

People often say that marriage requires a lot of hard work and compromise. I don't completely agree with that. In fact, if it's going to always be a lot of hard work – well – who wants that? We already work hard at our jobs! We work hard maintaining our homes. We work hard to be healthy, content individuals. Marriage shouldn't feel like a constant struggle or another hard job, and <u>won't</u>, when proper preparation and ground work has been done in advance.

Compromise is fine – to a point. But if you are constantly having to compromise on one thing or another, sooner or later you'll start to feel over-compromised, and then resentment will start to build. Don't get me wrong – there will be rough patches in any marriage or committed relationship, and these phases will require work.

Compromise will sometimes be necessary and mutual respect is a must. But, if you have seriously considered the questions and issues raised in this book, then conducted the seven essential conversations outlined – first with yourself, and then with your partner - you have already completed a significant part of the prep work for a successful marriage. Chances are that through these exercises you've found ways to compromise that will leave both parties feeling whole and secure.

If you regularly make time for meaningful discussions about what's happening in both your individual and united lives, together you'll create a bond of trust and intimacy that will get you through difficult times in a way that makes the relationship stronger.

Remember that we all bring different ideas to the table. We first learn about relationships from the home we grow up in. Typically, we tend to think that whatever rules and norms existed in our family of origin constitute "normal." If that is the case, then there are as many "normals" as there are families, because no two families are alike.

I often suggest to clients that a key privilege and responsibility we have as adults is to question everything we were taught as

children. Examine <u>all</u> the rules – social, religious, gender, political, financial, practical, what have you. Challenge them. Do
they make sense? Do they resonate with you and your values
today? If you are like most people, you will embrace much of
what you were taught; you absorbed the examples around you.
Be mindful that it is only when you challenge those values that
you can truly embrace them as your own, which is much wiser
and healthier than blindly and unconsciously adopting ideas
you inherited.

There will surely be rules or values that you choose to mod-
ify, or even throw out altogether. It is your prerogative to do
so (within the confines of the law, of course). The freedom
to make your own choices for your own family is a gift and
reward of adulthood. At the beginning of a new relationship,
you and your partner have a fabulous opportunity to explore
key issues together and create a new "normal" that works for
the two of you.

Marriages don't come with any guarantee. Even if you engage
in all the essential conversations and follow the suggestions
in this book, your relationship may end in divorce. People
sometimes simply choose the wrong mate; and people can and
do change. Rest assured, this is a good thing! Hopefully, we
all change and grow as we proceed on our respective journeys
through life. We mature and build character as we gain new
perspective from our experiences.

In the best of all worlds, couples move through various stages
of life on similar or parallel paths that enhance mutual growth;
but sometimes people change in ways that cause their paths to

diverge, rather than come together. If this happens, the skills you've developed by having these essential conversations will serve you well. You will navigate difficult waters with confidence and trust in both yourself, and your partner.

You are on the springboard of an exciting, challenging, and hopefully long, pleasing chapter of your life. While no relationship is guaranteed to be successful, you have taken important steps toward improving your odds of having an immensely happy future. By taking time to do your "due diligence" before making what is most likely the biggest decision of your life, you've given yourself and your mate the tools and training that will pave the way for a smooth, glorious ride ahead.

I wish you all the very best on your journey. May it be filled with love, joy, discovery, learning, and peace.

"After all these years, I see that I was mistaken about Eve in the beginning; It is better to live outside the Garden with her- than inside it without her."
Mark Twain

Lee A. Bowers, Ph.D., is a licensed psychologist in private practice in Villanova, PA. She has more than 30 years experience working with individuals, families and couples. To learn more about Dr. Lee or request a consultation, please visit her website at: **www.drleebowers.com**, e-mail: **leebowers@comcast.net**, or phone: 610-520-0443.

www.ingramcontent.com/pod-product-compliance
Lightning Source LLC
Chambersburg PA
CBHW060900280326
41934CB00007B/1123